WAR AND MORAL DISCOURSE

WAR
AND
MORAL
DISCOURSE

Ralph B. Potter

JOHN KNOX PRESS
Richmond, Virginia

Standard Book Number: 8042-0863-8
Library of Congress Catalog Card Number: 69-18111
© M. E. Bratcher 1969
Printed in the United States of America

To My Parents

PREFACE

The text of this volume bears marks of its origin. It was first prepared as a paper to be delivered at the annual meeting of The American Society of Christian Ethics in Kansas City, January 19, 1968. At that time, the war in Vietnam was being waged with high intensity and protests against the war were escalating sharply. The topic assigned to me was "New Problems for Conscience in War."

Months before the meeting I set out to prepare a scholarly treatise upon the just war doctrine. But throughout the year hardly a day went by without some individual or group calling upon me to strengthen their immediate efforts to remove the occasion of new problems for conscience in war by joining in some form of direct action. The persistence and variety of the requests required that I reconsider the priorities of my vocation as a professor of Christian ethics. While men were fighting and civilians were dying, how could I withdraw into the solitude and security of the Harvard College Library?

I was forced to ask myself, "What contribution can I best make to the cause of a stable peace? What are the most salient new problems of conscience of war *for me*, that is, for a churchman and a professor of ethics too old to fight and even too old to refuse to fight in the conflict in which our nation is engaged in Southeast Asia? As a teacher within the academic community, what priorities should I observe in the allocation of my energies? Should I abandon my academic post and seek a more immediate means of serving peace? Or, should I persevere in the neglected task of evaluating the reasoning processes by which men assess the rightness and wrongness of resort to war and conduct of war?"

The war in Vietnam has been a tragic affair. I feel obliged to do something. This sharp concern, which I share with so many others, might be disparaged in some theological circles as the paltry legacy of the bankrupt social gospel movement. But whatever its origin, the concern persists. It is not dispelled by reading the Gospels or by contemplating the injunction "Love thy neighbor." I am not put at ease when I hear Amos declare, "Woe to those who are at ease in Zion" (Amos 6:1, R.s.v.). What then shall an ethics professor do?

The opening sections of this book deal with the vocational dilemmas of the Christian ethicist who, in the midst of his academic responsibilities, is continually beset by the temptation to do something more dramatic, something that holds promise of more immediate impact upon policy and people. These reflections constitute a memo to my own divided will. I have, in effect, turned up the volume on my own internal dialogue as I go about deciding what I am to do under the constant pressure to do something helpful.

I believe that the ethicist can make a significant contribution by thinking, by thoughtful appropriation of past wisdom and imaginative projection of future demands. He can test presently fashionable habits of thought against the widest range of human experience and the highest standards of critical thought. If an ethicist can even slightly modify the formulae employed by policy makers in determining which factors are to be considered in policy formulation and what weight is to be assigned to each consideration, he can exercise an indirect yet important effect upon the conduct of public affairs. He can help reorder perception of the priorities to be attained in the common life. The ethicist can himself speak up and can often induce others to join him in saying to leaders, "Please reconsider your policy formulations in light of these significant considerations which have not been taken duly into account." Such modest and seemingly innocuous utterances can take on tremendous power when a resolute minority affirms neglected values and insists that concerns heretofore disregarded be given greater weight in policy formulation.

To reflect upon the full range of proper human concerns and the ways and means by which they may be balanced and interrelated is to perform a social function that can have revolutionary implications in a complacent setting and a cautionary, balancing effect upon revolutionary programs. Individuals, movements, and societies are prone to realize some interests and overlook others. Normative ethical thought that reasserts neglected claims can be a potent stimulus to the elaboration of more balanced and beneficial policies. Within his own calling, an ethicist may be deeply embroiled in a fundamental form of social action.

Most readers have no inclination to become professionally engaged in the academic discipline of ethics. Yet students facing vocational choices, pastors called upon to lead their congregations and communities in a variety of activities, housewives and laymen eager to make some contribution to the public good, all share dilemmas similar to the ethicist's quandary concerning the level of thought and action at which to invest time and energy. Likewise, all share an interest in the preservation of the clarity and power of moral discourse as a means of exerting nonviolent influence. Most particularly, all share a stake in the construction of moral restraints upon the use of violence.

The foremost motive in publishing this essay is the hope that readers of diverse background and training will be drawn further into the ancient and continuing discussion of the limits of the justifiable and the unjustifiable uses of violence. Here the focus is upon international relations. But the questions, the answers, and the reasoning processes have relevance also for moral reflection upon the use of violence in domestic affairs within nations. Commentators are challenged to give a coherent account of the limits of justifiable use of force that applies consistently to both the war in Vietnam and the outbursts of violence in American cities. Some condone and some condemn violence in both circumstances. But Hawks, who find the war to be morally defensible but are morally outraged by civil disorders, and Doves, who judge the war to be immoral but condone resort to violence in urban America, set for themselves the task of discriminating between justifiable and unjustifiable uses of violence. We wish to explore the bases on which such discrimination can be made with the greatest clarity and consistency.

The title of the essay has been changed from "New Problems for Conscience in War" to "War and Moral Discourse." A number of recent books on the morality of war bear the term "conscience" in their titles.[1] In replacing that term with an allusion to "moral discourse," I wish to emphasize that it is important to consider not only the question, How ought a well-formed conscience respond to the present dilemmas of war? but also, In what terms can we carry on a public discussion regarding right and wrong conduct in war? The legacy of Christians in America includes recurrent exemplifications of an ethic for saints and martyrs intent upon resisting war and refusing service as soldiers or as magistrates. But can Christians help to define an ethic for the policeman, the statesman, the conscientious combatant?

Men of conscience are obliged to do more than declare at a given moment that their sense of propriety has now been violated. They should expose the structure of thought that gives form to their conscience and should contribute day by day to the formation of a common conscience in the nation through persistent debate over the types of acts that may and may not be justified in the service of any cause, however just. It is morally irritating to see zealous moralists pass year after year without exerting themselves to clarify the moral dilemmas entailed in such questions as torture, ambush, sabotage, intervention, blockade, reprisal, asylum, the use of terror and the taking of hostages, and then hurl denunciations at military and political leaders who, under severe pressure of time and circumstance, make judgments which appear to be morally dubious. The moral problems of war and conduct in war require constant reflection and persistent public perusal. It is to be hoped that when peace breaks out in Southeast Asia, those who have been concerned with the morality of this particular war will persevere in discussion of two variants of the perennial question concerning the discrimination of justifiable and unjustifiable uses of violence in international relations: Under what circumstances is it immoral to wage war? and Under what circumstances is it immoral not to wage war?

In making slight revisions in the text, I have decided to preserve references to the war in Vietnam in the present tense appropriate January, 1968. Hopefully, by the time this volume appears in print, such references will seem curiously anachronistic. If occasional allusions seem dated, I hope, nevertheless, that the main argument will not be outdated. The central theme is that critical reflection upon the criteria for defining justifiable and unjustifiable applications of force will be a perennial moral obligation and political necessity in a world not purged of enmity and strife.

I wish to make special acknowledgment of the encouragement of my teacher, James Luther Adams; the counsel of my colleague, Arthur Dyck; and the loving-kindness of my wife, Jean. Among many helpers, they especially have been always present and constantly patient.

CONTENTS

1
TEMPTATIONS TO "RELEVANCE"

A sensitive American would find it difficult to be indifferent to the involvement of his nation in the war in Vietnam. Whether he be in opposition to or in support of our engagement and conduct in the war, there are many modes of action through which he may express his views and seek to influence opinion and policy. Students of Christian ethics who long for "relevance" and are not disposed to stand aloof from issues of public policies must determine the level of involvement at which they will choose to act. There are various levels of involvement open today. Among the most tempting options are to join in a variety of direct action projects; to apply for membership in the "social action curia" and seek to mobilize churchmen; to work as an archaeologist of the ethical tradition, digging up wisdom from the past; or to strive to become a poor man's Walter Lippmann, addressing a wider public as a theologically informed political pundit. Finally, one might choose to concentrate upon criticism of the modes of ethical reasoning or patterns of moral thought employed by churchmen and statesmen in thinking about matters of war and peace.

The American tradition of activism, popular theologies of "involvement," an urge for self-vindication, and the pressure of friends already engaged conspire to make involvement at the more concrete levels of direct action, mobilization, and relevant political commentary seem most pressing and rewarding. So many of us have become involved in such varied forms of activity that one is compelled to ask, "Is there anything that we do, or ought to do, precisely as Christian ethicists and not as activists, bureaucrats, historians, and publicists?" If we performed these latter roles to perfection, would there be any task left undone which is incumbent upon us as ethicists? Is there a distinct discipline of Christian ethics that should equip us to make a specific contribution to reflection upon issues of war and peace?

There is indeed a distinctive task that too often has been left undone. At present there is an unmet demand for rigorous analyses of the logic by which we as Christians and as citizens can appropriately apply the terms "good" and "bad" or "right" and "wrong" to decisions about war and peace.

It is fitting to be concerned for effective action at the more concrete levels of involvement. But operations in the more "practical" dimensions of the political process are grounded in commitments, values, beliefs, and arguments which are the subject of the ethicist's professional concern. His work is itself a contribution to the political process. Those active at other levels of involvement proceed on grounds established or undermined by the critical labors of the ethicist. Hence, if we consider carefully the prerequisites for effectiveness at the more concrete levels of involvement, we find that an ethicist eager for "relevance" should give highest priority to his own peculiar calling to make persistent inquiry into the cogency of reasons given for and against decisions, that is, in this case, reasons for and against the decision to participate in war. His skills are indispensable for those who seek continuing success in conducting demonstrations, mobilizing churchmen, renewing our moral and political legacy, or fulfilling the role of social critic.

1. *A Service to Demonstrators.* In many situations it is difficult and embarrassing not to become engaged in demonstrations protesting the war. Once enlisted, it is even more embarrassing and difficult to become disengaged. Demonstrations have their own logic of escalation; a point of diminishing returns can be reached when the public becomes inured. Arousing the conscience of the nation thereafter cannot be achieved by inventing more ingenious or intense forms of demonstration. It is contingent upon the reformation of conscience itself. That task requires emphasis upon more sustained modes of moral education which could create a sensitive and resonant public conscience.

2. *Facilitating Mobilization.* Leaders of social education and action agencies of the major denominations are masters of less demonstrative techniques of mobilizing churchmen. But again, in order to halt or mitigate the war, it would not be enough to marshal those who presently are persuaded of its injustice. Many others must be convinced that Christian conscience requires them to oppose the barbarities of war. That task requires not a more skillful administrative technique but a more profound critique of the terms and categories employed by churchmen in deciding which actions are most incumbent upon them.

But even if all American Protestants could be resensitized, mobilized, and allied with Christians of ecumenical disposition at home and abroad, their capacity to influence public affairs would not be equal to the scope and depth of the problems about which their faith requires them to be concerned. If churchmen take seriously the injunction to go into the world to serve both the near and the distant neighbor, they will find a globe inhabited by adherents of non-Christian religions who are now significant actors in what has become for the first time a common world history in which the destinies of nations are linked together in a new degree of interdependence. All men of goodwill must be enlisted in the cause of justice and peace. But how are they to be addressed and stirred to action? We cannot simply quote our own Scriptures or call upon them to emulate Jesus or appeal to the teaching authority of the church. God has allowed our political and geographical parochialism to be superceded. Our intellectual parochialism must be abandoned. Students of theological ethics can make an indispensable contribution to the common cause of humanity by renewing the search for a point of contact with the reason and conscience of men of traditions other than Protestantism or Christianity or Western humanism.

The continuing vitality of highly particularistic, confessional language poses a dilemma especially severe for proponents of Christocentric and contextualist systems of ethics. Latent zeal can still be released by appeals couched in fervently Christian terms. But there is danger that religious particularism will reinforce political provincialism and cultural xenophobia. But even if the faithful are motivated by Christian symbols to seek universal justice, the political power to accomplish the demands of justice has not been granted to the *koinonia*. This insufficiency in the practical order has implications for the Christian's mode of thinking and speaking about ethics. As I ponder the command of Christ, I conclude that love for my neighbor requires me to work for peace through participation in political movements. I cannot guide these movements by appeal to distinctively Christian categories.[2] I must find some surrogate for one version or another of the natural law tradition. Short of the sudden conversion of all men to Christ, peace can best be served by a mutual recovery of common moral law known to "men of sound reason." Only through the implementation of such a moral law can disparate groups establish a tolerable world order. And only if such a minimal order exists can there be a history within which the church, as the vanguard of the new humanity, continues its redemptive mission. The epistemological problems which have bedeviled attempts to refurbish the natural law tradition demand intense investigation by ethicists desirous of advancing the cause of love and justice within a world community.

3. *Retrieving Our Legacy.* Men of goodwill who seek a common moral law will still be puzzled about specific problems of conscience in war. But they need not start anew in pondering the dilemmas. There is a large deposit of wisdom buried in our libraries. Excavation of the several traditions can convince us that in a sense there are no new problems for conscience in war. In earlier centuries, men of great intellectual power have pondered moral questions pertaining to aggression, intervention, reprisals, hot pursuit, negotiations, diplomatic recognition, reparations, extradition, asylum, hostages, torture, prisoners of war, blockades, ambush, military necessity, use of poison, revolution, sabotage, sedition, espionage, treason, sanctuary, conscientious objection, and so forth. The problems we face are new only in the sense that under the nuclear umbrella they have emerged again to become salient. Our situation as ethicists seems new because other disciplines, chastened by events, have created a market for products of reasonable quality which we might be able to bring forth. Those who have explored the riches of the tradition have extracted great profit for modest labors. In human terms, for ethicists as for others, the war in Vietnam is a tragedy. But professionally, it is a reprieve from the suspicion that Christian ethicists have no helpful insight to contribute to debates over public policy. That which has been most helpful we have received as a gift from our intellectually assiduous ancestors.

4. *The Temptation of Punditry.* Historical research is useful. Exploration of the paths of reasoning pursued by our

forebears enables us to foresee where certain arguments may lead. But the tradition cannot provide us with perfect analogues or detailed prescriptions for policy choices confronting us today. Those who consider it to be their task as ethicists to dispense to believers and to magistrates timely instructions regarding the precise and proper content of public policy decisions tend to be impatient with prolonged reflection upon the major alternative modes of reasoning illumined for us in the traditional theological and ethical writings. Imbued with a perpetual sense of crisis, they may wish to exercise an immediate role in public deliberation by contending for or against pending proposals. The drift into political punditry and journalism is the besetting temptation of those trained in Christian ethics today.

A strange question intrudes itself upon one contemplating the range of literature produced by American Christians in the twentieth century on the morality of war, What should be the ethics of "doing ethics"? In the years since World War II virtually every prominent American theologian and ethicist has addressed himself in print to questions of war and peace. Prior to the escalation of the war in Vietnam, essays most frequently were opened with some variant of the observation that the threat of nuclear annihilation is the most serious problem confronting the world today. What conceit it must take to attack the most serious problem of the age in a single essay written with one's left hand. The complaint is not that such authors should do less and should leave the field to "experts," but that they should do much more to assist this generation in the search for appropriate answers by bringing to bear and expanding the wisdom available in the tradition of Western ethics and political philosophy. Mindful of the immense stakes at issue in the way men think and act about right and wrong in warfare, they should apply reasonable diligence before tinkering with the fundamental moral sanctions upon which our peace and security depend. The casualness with which men well disciplined in other fields have expressed themselves regarding the morality of war seems best explained by imputing to them an assumption that any good word for "peace" is helpful and that the function of ethicists is not to "speak the whole truth" regarding right and wrong in policy formulation, but only to provide a counterweight to the allegedly ferocious inclinations of incumbent administrations. No matter how irresponsible a government may be in its usurpation of moral commendations, counterexaggerations of the simplicity and certainty of moral judgments are not helpful.

In seeking "relevancy" through immediacy, ethicists, in addition to sins of commission wrought through slovenly analyses, have also committed sins of omission; they have left undone the task of careful public criticism of moral categories concerning right and wrong use of force that must be performed if the public is to attain an understanding of the rational restraints upon the use of force necessary to restrain violence at home and warfare abroad.

2

THE COMPLEXITY
OF POLICY
RECOMMENDATIONS

Most Christian ethicists are eager to be "relevant." It is frequently supposed that to be relevant one must advance or advocate specific recommendations for public policy. What authority can the ethicist claim at this level of endeavor?

Recommendations for what should be done here and now represent complex judgments. Every statement which proposes a policy by specifying a responsible agent, a goal, and an appropriate means for its realization is derived through a complex reasoning pattern which may conveniently be analyzed into four elements. In some cases, each element is made explicit. More frequently, one or more of the ingredients of policy thought are left implicit.

1. Every policy recommendation entails an *empirical definition of the situation,* a series of judgments concerning political and military facts and potentially falsifiable predictions concerning the outcomes of alternative courses of action.

2. *Affirmation of loyalty* also affects policy thought. Consciously or unconsciously, men make decisions regarding what shall be taken as their primary object of concern. They create expressive symbols which represent a center of value, locus of commitment, or source of identity. It

makes a difference whether they are dedicated to a nation, an ideology, a church, "humanity," an ideal community, or some other object of loyalty.

3. Policy thought requires a decision concerning the *mode of ethical reasoning* to be employed. What constitutes a good reason for choosing one course or another? What factors are to be taken into consideration? What priority and weight is to be given each?

4. Men's decisions are inevitably shaped by their *quasi theological beliefs* concerning God, man, and human destiny. Anthropological assumptions concerning the range of human freedom and man's power to predict and control historical events have particular importance.

The process of formulating policy inevitably entails implicit or explicit assumptions regarding all four factors in this analytical paradigm adapted from the general theory of action of the sociologist, Talcott Parsons.[3] Each of the four elements is independently variable; that is, even though certain patterns and systematic interrelations tend to recur, one cannot predict the final policy outcome or the content of any one element from knowledge of any combination of other factors. To understand the structure of policy thought, it is necessary to examine each of the four elements.

This observation is important when one is attempting to comprehend and describe contrasting policy views in the hope of discerning the origins of disagreement and determining the prospects for closer accord. Disagreement may begin within any or all of the four elements. For example, two commentators may stand firmly within the same theological tradition, employ the same ethical apparatus, agree upon the locus of ultimate commitment but come to diverse policy views because of variations in their definition of the situation stemming from differences in their patterns of access to and appropriation of empirical data. Conversely, two observers may acknowledge the same "facts," be devoted to the same "bearer of value," apply the same rules of ethical procedure, but stand opposed to each other in the realm of policy because all these shared ingredients are interpreted within disparate theological contexts. Or again, variations may begin in disagreement concerning the point at which the Christian should invest his ultimate loyalty— the community, visible or invisible, which should serve as his definitive reference group in moments of consideration and decision. Finally, diversity may have its roots in dispute over the proper procedure for determining ethical action— there may be alternative estimates of what factors are to be considered and what weight they are to be given in the process of deciding.

Policy thought is exceedingly complex. It is not deduced from theological axioms, determined by habits of moral reasoning, derived from affectional loyalties, nor drawn from simple knowledge of circumstances. Perfect ecumenical accord upon theological and ecclesiastical questions would not eradicate the variety of responses to political issues evident among Christians. Nor would the sudden triumph of one form of ethical reasoning or common affirmation of the vision of humanity or complete unanimity concerning political and military facts suffice to induce settlement of disputes concerning the proper course of policy. Those who agree firmly regarding one of these elements may yet disagree sharply regarding policy. Yet, conversely, men who disagree regarding each of the separate elements may converge and agree on what policy is to be pursued. It can be factually startling but not theoretically surprising that "in politics there are strange bedfellows."

Three implications of this paradigmatic analysis of the structure of policy recommendations are of particular interest.

1. There can be no "non-moral view" of political or military affairs. Secular strategists may prefer to avoid the traditional vocabulary of moral discourse, but they cannot avoid making assumptions regarding ethical methods and norms. It should be part of the business of the Christian ethicist to ferret out these ethical assumptions and expose them to public scrutiny. If General X or his civilian advisor states that escalation would be good policy, we should ask, Why? What makes it good? If we ask the question Why? persistently, proponents must eventually move from conventional legitimations of policy in terms of "national interest" towards a more general and systematic analysis of the modes of justifying conduct and finally, to reflection upon the basic purposes of human existence and civil community.[4] Such questioning will ultimately raise the issue, Who is truly competent to judge what is good for man and society?[5]

2. There can be no "purely moral view" of policy. No detailed recommendations flow simply and directly from the realm the ethicist commands as an ethicist. Authorities in the field of ethics share the plight of other experts. When they move beyond the limited area of their own special competence to formulate policy recommendations, they must, at their own risk, incorporate data drawn from the realm of other men's expertise. Their professional authority is adulterated and they properly become subject to the critical scrutiny of disciplined experts and undisciplined laymen.

Some may claim that as ethicists their competence, like that of the philosopher-king, is precisely that of combining all four elements into determining prudent policy. Political pundits reduce the discipline of ethics to casuistry, to the assessment of right policy in specific cases. The product of political casuistry is political wisdom. But who is competent to evaluate wisdom and accredit the aspiring casuist? No graduate program offers a degree in political wisdom. The casuist cannot receive credentials from fellow ethicists. Only the public itself can validate the claim that recommendations will prove wise in living the common life. No expert, trained in one of the several elements of policy thought, can claim to have the comprehensive competence to guide political choices. Each can only contribute his expert knowledge, explicate the reasons for his preferences, and submit his case for the consideration of all the people who together must make decisions that should never be relinquished to the potential tyranny either of the despot or of the expert.

Churchmen and ethicists should, as citizens, participate fully in the political process. But they should resist the temptation to practice "cheap prophecy." If they wish to be "prophetic" and risk the accretion of an aura of divine inspiration and commission, they should proclaim boldly, "Thus saith the LORD" and take the prophet Micaiah, whose deeds are recorded in 1 Kings 22, as the model of their prophetic careers. Micaiah, in contradicting the aspirations of King Ahab and the unanimous testimony of 400 false prophets, had the courage and confidence to make his prophecy falsifiable and submit it to the test of experience: "If you return in peace, the Lord has not spoken by me" (1 Kings 22:28, R.S.V.). He put his body on the line and languished in prison while his inspired word was tested. Such specificity and candor would be refreshing and would enable prophetic pundits to approximate the canons of responsibility they impose upon the incumbent policy makers whose wisdom they seek to supplant.

3. An alternative mode of influence which capitalizes upon the distinctive skills of the ethicist is suggested by the third implication of our paradigmatic analysis. The ele-

ments of policy thought are systematically interrelated. If, then, one brings about a significant change in one sector, the entire pattern will be modified. The ethical element is a particularly potent source of change, for it largely determines the logical structure of a chain of policy argument and the weight to be assigned to the considerations deemed pertinent. To change the way men think about what is right and wrong in the conduct of political and military affairs is to exert a powerful, if somewhat indeterminant, influence upon the course of policy. While ethicists have been engaged in other tasks, they have left this possibility relatively unexploited, or in some cases have disparaged the contribution their own discipline might make to the process of formulating policy.

It is true that refinement of ethical analysis which permits more precise identification of factors properly to be considered as right- and wrong-making characteristics of particular actions and policies will not in itself yield unanimous certitude regarding what is to be done in particular instances. The distinctively ethical element is only one ingredient in policy thought. The policy recommendations which flow from the complex reasoning process will vary according to differences of input from the other three quadrants of our paradigm. No single element can alone be determinative. Hence, it is silly to dismiss the work of the ethicist as "irrelevant" just because immediate conclusions regarding policy do not flow from his evaluations of various modes of thinking about conduct in war. It would be just as silly to derogate or ignore the work of empirical data collectors simply because their factual reports do not automatically, in and of themselves, settle the question of what is to be done. A prudent policy maker requires the best empirical data possible; he also needs careful and critical ethical analyses.

Ethicists do not have to depart from their professional calling in order to make a significant contribution to the direction and correction of the political process. An example of the influence that an ethicist may wield through the performance of his professional role can be adduced. Members of the discipline of ethics have sought to influence policy regarding the war in Vietnam through involvements on each level we have mentioned. But if we ask which member has made the greatest contribution to the cause of those who oppose the war, the ironic answer would have to be Paul Ramsey. It is Ramsey who has been most responsible for restoring to public consciousness the traditional criteria of the just war which, as the debate has become more pointed and precise, have come increasingly to be utilized as the most effective categories for public discussion regarding the limits of morally justifiable resort to force.[6] Ramsey's contributions as a casuist have had less wide appeal. But through application of his skill as an ethicist in the narrower sense, he has helped to set an appropriate agenda for rational public debate and has thereby served the public good and contributed to the cause of justice and peace a gift of intellectual guidance which could come from no other discipline.

3

USES
AND ABUSES
OF MORAL DISCOURSE

Whatever else we may choose to do, ethicists bear the obligation of defending the clarity and precision of moral discourse. All citizens have a high stake in preserving the possibility of moving others through the use of moral language which constitutes the most nonviolent mode of influence. People do things with moral terms. They are tools or weapons with which we can goad the lethargic or restrain the unreflective. When moral terms are misused, when the tool of speech is blunted and the nonviolent weapon is rendered ineffective, men are more likely to resort to cruder, more lethal weapons. Hence, the beginning of moral responsibility is the preservation of the possibility of serious moral discourse. A government that distorts or mishandles words and concepts does a disservice to the cause of peace and humanity. Likewise, protestors who abandon sobriety and rational debate betray the cause they profess.

There are several modes of misuse of moral argument which severely jeopardize the prospects for edifying discourse.[7]

1. One abuse is to remove reasoning processes from critical scrutiny and bombard fellow citizens with continual declarations of conscience rather than provide closely rea-

soned moral arguments. By this technique conclusions are proposed as axioms. Those unable to perceive the presumed self-evidence of such affirmations are not instructed in the reasoning process by which they might come to share these convictions. Without such explication, these declarations are a self-deceptive means of evading rather than fulfilling responsibility for the promotion of civil debate. To be most helpful, statements should include explanatory as well as exhortatory materials.

2. A second means of undermining the utility of moral discourse is to ignore the test of generalizability.[8] We must ask whether the categories and principles invoked in argument about the war in Vietnam will prove equally acceptable when applied to other situations in which one must assess the justifiability of resort to violence. One might argue against the war in Vietnam on the simple principle that "nations should not intervene in the internal affairs of other regions or states." But anyone making such an argument doubtless became aware of its danger in June, 1967, if he happened to be an ardent supporter of the state of Israel. Other men of liberal sentiment should be careful not to commit themselves now to principles that would require them later to stand idly by as witnesses to a war of extermination waged against the black people of South Africa by a regime insured of impunity by principles presently upheld rigorously by earnest but short-sighted moralists.

If the principles by which resort to violence may be judged justifiable or unjustifiable are to pass the test of generalizability, they must be capable of being applied impartially to assess the moral legitimacy of the war in Vietnam, resort to violence by urban slum dwellers in the United States, and behavior of domestic police forces. A burden of proof is cast upon those who would condemn resort to violence in some cases and justify it in others. They must indicate how the cases differ in some relevant respect which permits variation in the judgment of what constitutes permissible behavior. The principle of generalization establishes that "what is right for one person must be right for every *relevantly* similar person in *relevantly* similar circumstances," or "what is right for one person cannot be wrong for another, unless there is some relevant difference in their natures or circumstances. Or, what is right (or wrong) for one person must be right (or wrong) for everyone, if there is no reason for the contrary."[9] The principle of generalizability requires explicit bases upon which exception to general rules may be assessed.

In discriminating between different circumstances in which resort to violence may or may not be justified, the traditional criteria of the "just war doctrine," to be explicated below, specify the relevant bases for distinguishing between cases and thereby permitting conduct in some instances that would be condemned in other situations.

Principles must be formulated and invoked with care. If men continually deny or reformulate their principles in order to derive the desired answer in each new situation, they subvert the seriousness of moral discourse. The concept of "reversibility" provides a convenient test for principles one is inclined to propose. A thoughtful arguer might ask, "Would I be willing to live under the rules I am promulgating if they were to be applied to me by others?" One effect of the principle of generalizability is "to throw a definite *onus probandi* on the man who applies to another a treatment of which he would complain if applied to himself."[10]

3. A third abuse is to despise the demand for consistency. There are different modes of ethical reasoning. Different things can be done with different approaches. Highly indeterminant approaches which rely upon situationally determined characterizations of acts as pragmatically "effec-

tive" or intuitively "fitting" are exceedingly useful to those
intent upon asserting autonomy and independence from
traditional norms of conduct. But to gain moral leverage for
restraining willful men, more codified systems presuming
to prescribe acts known in advance to be "right" or "obed-
ient" through the power of reason or the authority of Scripture or church are more useful. In recent years the trend,
both in literature and in popular fancy, has been toward the
less prescriptive, more intuitive and situational approach.

Students of the sociology of knowledge might suggest
that the adoption of certain modes of ethical reasoning is related to their perceived utility in dealing with the types of
issues that appear most salient in successive periods. Not so
long ago sex was the big issue on campus. Young people,
eager to gain freedom from traditional restraints, disclaimed
all moralizing interference with individual autonomy. They
ridiculed the idea of moral absolutes and the notion that certain acts could be inherently wrong. They helped dismantle
the traditional apparatus of natural law which had provided leverage for restraining those disinclined to acknowledge a law higher than their own utility. They embraced
situational ethics and proclaimed that henceforth we could
rely upon intuitive perception of the demands of love in
each isolated situation.

Times change. The big issue now is war. Where is
Joseph Fletcher this year?[11] Young people are not suddenly
eager to be restrained. But they would like to know how to
impose moral restraint in the conduct of war. Having cleared
away the barriers to free operation of intuition, they are
alarmed by the content of other men's intuition concerning
what love requires of us in Southeast Asia. The equipment
for reconstructing moral restraints is available in our tradition. But it seems no one under thirty knows how to make
the intellectual apparatus work.

Utter freedom in the private sphere can be purchased only at the cost of allowing other men license in the public sphere. It is dangerous to adopt a mode of ethical reasoning before testing its implications for the entire range of human concerns and circumstances, because styles of argument cannot be adopted and abandoned at one's convenience without making the institution of morality appear to be merely a means for self-serving rationalization. The utility of moral discourse is undermined by such inconsistency. The ethicist must help prevent such a circumstance by conducting a continuous public inquiry into the cogency of the reasons offered in justification of conduct.

4
"ILLEGAL, IMMORAL, AND UNJUST"

In the present context, in order to fulfill their professional obligation to question the cogency of reasons offered in justification of conduct, ethicists must ask the administration, "If the war in Vietnam is justifiable, why is it so?" They must also pose to opponents of the war the question, "If the war is wrong, why is it wrong?"

A standard formula for condemnation is that the war is "Illegal, immoral, and unjust." The indictment is not redundant. The terms have distinguishable meanings which are, from the side of the state, increasingly compelling.

1. The method utilized to demonstrate the illegality of the war is to compare the behavior of the United States with specification of acts expressly forbidden and condemned in treaties, conventions, accords, and judgments held to be legally binding upon the nation and upon individual citizens.[12] The binding force of international law in an international society devoid of enforcement agencies is a matter of continuing controversy.[13] Even if it were determined beyond a doubt that the present acts of the United States violate every canon of international law, one could still question whether this consideration alone would, could, or should have an appreciable effect upon policy. To suggest that the legality of an act should have a determinative effect

upon policy formation requires the prior moral assumption "that which is illegal ought not to be done." This principle has been effectively undermined not only by our revolutionary forefathers but more recently with the frequent endorsement of liberal churchmen, by civil rights demonstrators, and by anti-war protestors themselves. It smacks of a legalism much maligned by popular writers on ethics in all other contexts.

Given the long-range desirability of an international system ruled by law, there must be a strong moral and political presumption against committing acts held to be violative of international law. The effect of policy upon the growth of respect for international law must be a consideration in the formulation of policy. But the asserted illegality of conduct does not itself constitute a sufficient reason to dismiss a proposed course of action. The maxim, "That which is illegal ought not to be done," cannot readily be imposed upon the state, which throughout its history has claimed the immunity of "necessity" and the privilege of putting aside conventional legal restraints when the existence or welfare of the nation is held to be in jeopardy. We have grown accustomed to individual and group appeals to a higher law. The state also claims a higher law—the law of its own survival. The charge that the war is illegal does not establish a firm restraint upon policy.

2. The legality of an act is a consideration to be weighed or overweighed in appraising its morality. But the determination that a war is "immoral" entails calculations beyond the verdict that it is illegal. The assertion that the war is not only "illegal" but also "immoral" may be more embarrassing but is also less definite in its connotations for different hearers. What can it mean to assert that a state has acted immorally?

a. Christians have perennially had difficulty in specifying norms appropriate for the civil community and its governing regime. It seems extravagant for Christians to demand perfect performance of the law of love from a secular institution composed partially of those who have not taken upon themselves the yoke of obedience to Christ. Indeed, in a pluralistic society, it is presumptuous and no doubt futile to impose even the less rigorous biblical norms which might be extracted from the epistles or from the practice of the Old Testament worthies. In the context of public debate concerning national policy, it is not helpful to take "immoral" to mean "in contradiction to standards revealed in Scripture or promulgated by the authority of a particular religious community." If that is what the term means, most political leaders and many among the populace will not blush at the charge that their nation has been "immoral."

b. The term may be interpreted to mean "in violation of certain reasonable rules of right conduct." But which rules are reasonable? How are they derived? What gives them binding authority? Who is to be judged competent to determine what reason requires?

c. "Immoral" may be understood by some to mean "offensive to the sense of propriety of a qualified moral observer." But again, in the political setting in which the question of morality has been raised as a means of gaining leverage to move the course of policy, the obvious question is, Who is to be accredited as a "qualified moral observer"? We have a variety of subcultures within which the sense of what is fitting may be formed differently. Whose sense is then to prevail in the formation of public policy? Or how can conflicting senses be harmonized or accommodated?

d. Another interpretation of "immoral" would take it to signify "that which will result in undesirable consequences." But then we must inquire, Consequences for whom? Over what span of time? What makes the consequences desirable or undesirable? In the present context, there is a practical disutility in employing the utilitarian approach as the basis for moral protest of the war. Given the necessity for a global estimate of the long-range consequences of policy for our nation's intricate involvements throughout the world, who can claim to be better qualified to provide the crucial calculations of benefits and costs than an incumbent administration? Moreover, this style of reasoning forecloses the claim that we do not need all the facts to know that the acts being performed in war are immoral. By this account, no act can be immoral in itself, no type of conduct can be condemned in advance since even the most hideous act, if viewed in the broadest perspective, might be calculated to serve the greatest good for the greatest number through time. An act of war may be "evil" in the sense of entailing great suffering, but if it can be judged to be the "lesser evil," it is tragic but obligatory. A lesser evil is not "evil" in the sense of being morally "wicked."[14] Such an act can be performed, perhaps with a heavy heart but still with good conscience, if by "immoral" we mean "resulting in a net balance of undesirable consequences."

In whatever metaethical framework the charge is made, the assertion that the war in Vietnam is "immoral" translates into the dictum, "The war ought not to be prosecuted, or at least not in the present manner." The utterance is made as a mode of influencing others, of encouraging them and giving them reason to oppose the war.

Many hearers are not moved by the simple declaration that the war is immoral. They persist in asking Why? or even So what? To move them from their obduracy, it is necessary to give a more thorough explication of the reasoning upon which the charge of "immoral" is based, an explication that will demonstrate that something more is at

stake than the ventilation of particular political predis-
positions. The moral reasoning employed must be shown to
be capable of rendering generalizable norms when applied
consistently to the full range of imaginable uses of force.
Metaethical questions impose themselves upon those who
invoke moral arguments in the hope of marshaling sentiment for or against a war because variation in moral judgment is one source of disagreement concerning policy, and
disparity in the mode of ethical reasoning is, in turn, one
source of disaccord in the content of moral judgments.

Variations in modes of ethical reasoning which may
seem exceedingly subtle to laymen are not so troublesome
when critics of diverse backgrounds are joined in opposition to a policy which they each may label "immoral," al-
beit for different reasons. But the significance of their diversity in habits of moral thought becomes more evident
when the prospect of a policy change creates a demand for
positive policy recommendations. Latent disagreements
then become manifest; alliances crumble as those who made
common cause against that which was seen as "immoral"
now must help to define a new, "moral" course. To establish the grounds for continued cooperation, it is necessary
to explore persistently the bases for moral judgments
through reflection upon metaethical questions concerning
the meaning, use, and binding power of moral language.

3. Critical reflection upon the processes of ethical reasoning is indispensable to effective political criticism and
construction. But, if those concerned about right and wrong
in warfare are not to get bogged down in a metaethical mo-
rass, it is useful to focus discussion upon the species of moral
judgment most immediately relevant to moral assessment of
the conduct of the state. Justice is the measure of political
action. In the debate concerning the propriety of the war,
the biggest "pay-off" is to be gained from concentration

upon that species of ethical reflection which, by inquiring into the justice of public acts, deals specifically with the norms of the conduct of the state. In the formula "illegal, immoral, and unjust," the crucial element is the assertion that the war in Vietnam is "unjust." The state, to be a state, is bound to do that which is just and to desist from that which is unjust. Otherwise, its citizens are absolved of their moral duty to serve and to obey and are, indeed, obliged to seek its reconstitution. The charge that the war is unjust is crucial because it invokes the strongest sanctions that can be brought to bear upon a political body.

Opposition to the war is most powerful when couched in terms of justice and injustice. Not everyone, however, is familiar with the language of justice. Protestant ethicists have devoted relatively little attention to explicating the demands of justice. Moreover, the metaethical controversies which bedevil attempts to arrive at agreement on that to be adjudged "immoral" reappear among those who hold conflicting theories concerning the nature of justice. "Justice" may refer to "conformity to the law," "doing what is useful for the social good," or "rendering to each what is his own and/or due by right."[15]

There are different theories concerning the precise meaning of the term "unjust." Common to all definitions is the idea that an unjust act violates an important and appropriate norm of civil behavior. But which norms are to be considered important and appropriate? For our purposes, the most helpful approach would be to proceed inductively in search of norms actually used by citizens in considering whether a particular resort to force is just or unjust. What norms of justice are commonly applied in practice? On what bases do conscientious observers render the judgment that a war is "immoral" in the specific sense of being "unjust"?

5

WHEN IS A WAR "UNJUST"?

How do people use the terms "just" and "unjust" in speaking about war? Is there a degree of concurrence, a common usage which transcends difference in the underlying theories of justice? What does it commonly mean to say that a war is "unjust"?

I have not completed a scientific content analysis of a defined sample of documents. But is seems that when stripped of elaborations and rhetorical flourishes, the arguments presented by various critics in support of the accusation that the war in Vietnam is "unjust" may be summarized as follows:

1. The United States intervened on behalf of one faction embroiled in a civil war. There was, prior to our massive buildup of forces, no clear aggression by a foreign power across established international boundaries. Hence, this is not an occasion of legitimate self-defense and there is no *justifying cause* for our action.

2. The war is unjust because all means of conciliation have not been exhausted and intimations of a willingness to negotiate have been spurned. Hence, the sharp escalation of military action cannot be justified as a *last resort*.

3. The war is not being conducted under the auspices of the *highest lawful authority*. South Vietnam is not an in-

dependent, sovereign state. Its government is not truly representative. The United Nations, as the highest world public authority, has not authorized military action.

4. No *announcement* of the intention to begin hostilities or clear stipulation of the conditions under which they might be avoided has been made to the enemy.

5. The United States has plunged in where there is *no reasonable hope of victory*. The leaders of North Vietnam have not been intimidated in the manner predicted by the projection of Western ideas of a rational cost/benefit calculation. Guerrillas in the South can persist indefinitely in disrupting programs of pacification.

6. We have not acted with *just intentions*. Even if suspicions of economic greed and neo-imperialist ambitions are discounted, our leaders have made it clear that we are not simply defending innocent South Vietnamese from the onslaught of an unjust external aggressor. Part of our intention is to preserve American prestige and to demonstrate the credibility of promises to our allies and threats to our enemies. The devastated land is being sacrificed to our geopolitical interest in containing Red China.

7. Our expenditure of men and money exceeds the limits of *due proportion*. The good to be accomplished in that small, strategically irrelevant corner cannot balance the evil that is being done to the Vietnamese, to all combatants, to our domestic tranquility, and to the status of the United States in world opinion.

8. The conduct of the war has not been confined to *just means*. Through the use of napalm, area bombing and the destruction of crops, we have been guilty of indiscriminant attacks upon innocent noncombatants. We have condoned, if not practiced, the use of torture.

In order to combat these arguments, those disposed to justify the war must either demonstrate that these consider-

ations are morally irrelevant or offer alternative interpreta-
tions of facts pertinent under each of these headings. No
simple agreement upon the substantive issue of the justifiability of the war emerges from tacit acceptance of these
points as an agenda for debate. But the distillation of these
criteria represents significant progress towards commonly
acknowledged rules for the right application of the term
"unjust." The criteria make it possible to specify the reasons
why a particular war may be condemned as unjust. This
well explicated and highly differentiated list of morally relevant considerations can be used consistently to yield generalizable conclusions on the limits of justifiable use of force.

This compendium of considerations has broad appeal
because it incorporates criteria appropriate to many different theories of justice and morality. It is a philosophically
untidy amalgam of questions pertaining to the past, present,
and future, that is, to the occasion, conduct, and consequences of war. It inquires into the form, motive, and consequences of acts. Teleological and dispositional criteria
are combined with formal, procedural requirements in a
manner which respects both the need and the limit of prudential calculation undertaken with regard for the idiosyn-
crasies of the particular situation. But the bedrock is an
apodictic commandment given by God and confirmed by
natural reason, "You shall do no murder."

Christian ethics grounded in loving obedience to divine
command converges here with ethical thought based upon
natural reason. Murder must never be done. Murder is unjustifiable homicide. But when is homicide unjustifiable?
When it is not done for a justifiable cause, as a last resort,
under lawful authority, through due process of law, with
reasonable hope of preserving justice, or when it escapes
limits of due proportion and is performed indiscriminately
without respect to means.

The elements in this definition of murder recapitulate the traditional criteria of the just war transmitted through the main line of Christian thinkers from Ambrose and Augustine, to Aquinas and the late scholastics, to the Reformers and Grotius and the founders of modern international law.[16] Common acceptance of these criteria by Christians and by secular men of discriminating moral sense would constitute a very significant moral and political fact. Intimations that such a convergence of moral sense is possible have stirred renewed interest in the often disparaged Christian teaching concerning justifiable war.

6

CHRISTIAN ATTITUDES TOWARD WAR AND PEACE

In many quarters there is a new disposition to inquire, What is the "just war doctrine"? Conventional answers accept the typology lucidly explicated by Roland Bainton and treat the just war doctrine alongside pacifism and the crusade as one of the three recurring Christian attitudes toward war and peace.

Broadly speaking, three attitudes to war and peace were to appear in the Christian ethic: pacifism, the just war, and the crusade. Chronologically they emerged in just this order. The early Church was pacifist to the time of Constantine. Then, partly as a result of the close association of Church and state under this emperor and partly by reason of the threat of barbarian invasions, Christians in the fourth and fifth centuries took over from the classical world the doctine of the just war, whose object should be to vindicate justice and restore peace. The just war had to be fought under the authority of the state and must observe a code of good faith and humanity. The Christian elements added by Augustine were that the motive must be love and that monks and priests were to be exempted. The crusade arose in the high Middle Ages, a holy war fought under the auspices of the Church or of some inspired religious leader, not on behalf of justice conceived in terms of life and property, but on behalf of an ideal, the Christian faith. Since the enemy was without the pale, the code tended to break down.[17]

Commentators differ radically in appraising the validity and relevance of the just war doctrine. Pacifists look upon it as a sub-Christian vestige of the Constantinian age, a smooth device by which a fallen church can rationalize nationalistic ambitions and accommodate itself to the necessities of worldliness. They charge that it has been an ineffective restraint upon war. Conversely, crusaders resent the possibility that restraints demanded by teachings on the just war might be effective enough to thwart their vigorous imposition of righteousness upon a recalcitrant world. Both pacifists and crusaders agree that the subtleties of just war thought should be rooted out of public consciousness and replaced with a simpler logic designed to maximize either the pacifist's ideal of love or the crusader's cause of freedom.

Even strong advocates of the validity and relevance of the just war doctrine suffer some discomfiture in attempting to apply the traditional criteria to the extraordinary forms of war for which the nations today prepare. They defend the historic evolution of the theory as a right and proper definition of the form that Christian love must take when confronted with the possibility of protecting the innocent from unjust attack. But the present prospect of attack and counterattack with multimegaton nuclear weapons makes modern warfare a less credible expression of agape in action. Some just war theorists strive to uphold the possibility of justifying certain forms of nuclear war, either by stretching the principle of double effect or by dispensing with the inconvenient condemnation of direct, purposeful attack upon the innocent.[18] Others apply all the criteria and conclude that modern war cannot be justified.[19] What then? That is the interesting question. What must happen when those who accept the just war doctrine apply its criteria and decide that the military policy of our nation is unjustifiable either in Vietnam or in deployment of weapons of mass destruction?

The obvious answer is that those who reach such conclusions must seek to change national policy. But how? And how soon? Given a sense of extreme urgency, the just war doctrine can yield an imperative to launch a revolution or to resort to tyrannicide. Less violent resistance may take the form of selective conscientious objection, tax refusal, and various applications of civil disobedience and noncooperation. More conventional modes of political action may be employed to seek specific changes of policy, perhaps to the point of unilateral disarmament and reliance on nonviolent resistance to potential invaders. Or, attention may be focused upon the long-range task of reordering the human community. Recent papal spokesmen reflecting upon *Pacem In Terris* have discovered a "structural defect" in the system of nation states and have turned their thoughts to *Populorum Progressio*. The moral agony of present circumstances may be relieved by laboring for the upbuilding of worldwide public authority invested with power to promote prosperity and preserve peace.

These varying responses can all be occasioned by application of the just war doctrine as a valid and relevant mode of thinking about current military policy and conduct. But what validity and relevance does the just war doctrine have for assessing the morality of action flowing from these various responses themselves? In assessing their own forms of resistance, are not those who oppose an "unjust war" bound to observe the same criteria they have invoked as the measure of morally tolerable action?

Those questions expose the unfortunate inaccuracy of the title and the narrow interpretation it imposes. Rightly perceived, the criteria of the "just war doctrine" pertain to all situations in which the use of force must be contemplated as an immediate or remote possibility. One disservice of Bainton's memorable typology is its tendency to reinforce the identification of the just war doctrine with the single problem of "war" conceived as an international conflict within a system of nation states. This obscures the relevance of the mode of thinking for assessing the use of domestic police power, revolutionary war, and war in a revolutionized world in which international peace-keeping forces may have to contend with new forms of civil war within the international community. Whenever men think about the morally responsible and therefore politically purposeful use of force, some analogue to the just war doctrine emerges, whether it be in non-Western cultures or in the Christian subculture.

Within the Christian community the just war doctrine evolved in response to two questions that arose first in a *pastoral* context in which conscientious believers, hoping to create a well-formed Christian conscience, inquired, In what circumstance may I, in good conscience, participate in the use of force? When there is proper occasion, what forms of force may I employ?[20] Refinement of the criteria given in answer to the first question and their transmission through the conscience of Christian magistrates into the political theory and international law of Western nations has led to the development of the *jus ad bellum,* the law which seeks to regulate resort to war. Reflection upon the second question has endowed our heritage with the *jus in bello,* the law of war which defines acts licit in the conduct of war.

These two elements, both of which are essential to the just war doctrine, have tended to fly apart in theory and practice. In the nineteenth century, international lawyers despaired of imposing the *jus ad bellum* upon sovereign and equal states and, unable to restrict the right to wage war, sought to meliorate war through the elaboration of the *jus in bello* in treaties and conventions signed at the Hague and in Geneva.[21] The American tradition, in contrast, has been grounded in an implicit affirmation of the *jus ad bellum.* A nation should resort to arms only in defense of an uncontrovertibly just cause. But once drawn into war in response to the wickedness of enemies, we have shown a disinclination to be bound by the fine distinctions of the *jus in bello*.[22] The challenge confronting contemporary exponents of the just war doctrine is to demonstrate how these two elements can be conjoined in moral theory, public consciousness, and political practice.

When we consider these two underlying questions which Christians cannot avoid even if they choose to be marginal participants in civil society, we may see that pacifism, the just war theory, and the crusade can be placed along a single continuum as differing answers to the same basic inquiry concerning the limits of Christian participation in the use of force. In a broad sense, all Christians have a just war doctrine, or a theory concerning the justifiable use of force. Some operate with a very simple set of criteria. Others employ more elaborate forms of reasoning designed to deal with a great variety of circumstances. As presupposed in our paradigm, the independently variable decisions regarding ultimate loyalties and theological beliefs exercise a strong systematic influence upon the elaboration of the ethical system.

Pacifists, who hold certain beliefs regarding the mission of the church and the distinctive calling of the Christian, profess to know ahead of time that a believer can never participate in the use of violence.[23] The need for subtle forms of ethical reasoning is foreclosed by the conviction that the issues are not subtle. Doing violence in any form is incompatible with Christian discipleship. These affirmations constitute simple, forthright replies to the two basic questions: When may I, in good conscience, participate in the use of force? Never. What forms of violence may I employ? None.

Crusading Christians have felt that these crisp criteria are too simple and require the faithful to leave undone many things that ought to be done out of charitable concern for the welfare of others. When the conception of what ought to be done through the application of the power of the state comes to include promotion of righteousness rather than mere restraint of specific acts of injustice, the crusading mentality appears. It erodes the *jus in bello* and applies in utilitarian fashion the single criterion of a just cause supplemented by prudent willingness to observe an economy of force. When may I participate in the use of force? When the true welfare of the people is to be served. What forms of violence may I employ? Any necessary for achieving the just cause.

The currently fashionable flirtation of Protestants with theories that portray violent revolution as a justifiable recourse for the urban ghetto dweller or the oppressed of underdeveloped nations reflects the recrudescence of crusading sentiment in a new guise. Violence is justified as a last resort in the service of a just cause. It is implied that extreme duress relieves the oppressed of the obligation to observe restraints imposed by the other criteria. Only prudent regard for world opinion and the sensitivities of those who might aid the revolution functions as a brake upon immediately advantageous violence. A generous concern for the dispossessed is admirable. But easy justifications are mischievous in a moral and political universe in which men must simultaneously contemplate how restraints are to be imposed upon international and counterrevolutionary forms of violence.

The system of thought referred to in the narrow sense as the just war doctrine incorporates both a strong pacifist longing to avoid killing and the crusader's commitment to a task to be accomplished among worldly men. This complex reasoning pattern is incomprehensible to those who have no abhorrence of killing and to those who are able to withdraw from the world or to suppose that they have a spiritual technique of fulfilling responsibilities of the common life.

Two types of claims are laid against the debt of love that Christians owe to their neighbors. These two claims establish the opposite poles of the continuum of Christian attitudes towards war and violence. One pole is established by the demand that we should not harm any neighbor. We should honor the example of Christ and do no violence in our own cause. But Christians have also recognized a claim created by the demand to protect the innocent, to lay down one's life for one's neighbor. The vindication of justice requires that self-sacrifice take the form of contending with evil men for the preservation of their intended victims. In different circumstances, self-sacrificing love of neighbor may find expression in strikingly different modes of conduct.

Moral power belongs to those who affirm both the obligation to contend for justice and the ideal not to harm. The two claims must be held together. But the effort to honor both demands creates a tension which underlies the dilemma that Christians must face in contemplating resort to violence. The two duties seem to draw in opposite directions. There is a constant temptation to relieve the tension by scanting one claim or the other and thus by simplifying the moral situation. Thus, some believers affirm the ideal of not harming but withdraw into passive resignation and desert the innocent to the depredations of unjust foes. Their concern for moral purity can bear the scent of sublimated selfishness, and their righteousness the taint of self-righteousness. Others become crusaders for justice and put aside all restrictions upon means. The destruction of the wicked becomes for them an occasion for glee rather than a tragic concession to the necessity of sparing the innocent. The style of thought employed by right wing advocates of sharp escalation in Vietnam and by left wing prophets of revolution in the ghettos is basically the same. In each case, a just cause is taken as a license to spurn inquiry regarding the moral legitimacy of means to be employed.

The just war doctrine provides a framework within which the two polar claims may be acknowledged through compromise. The ideal of not harming is affirmed even though the exercise of forceful means is condoned in exceptional circumstances to protect the innocent and to vindicate justice. There is, however, another style of thought and action which holds the two demands firmly together in a manner which commands profound moral respect. The nonviolent philosophy espoused and exhibited by Martin Luther King, Jr., and his disciples attempts to preserve the moral tension between the two poles. Dr. King knew the demands of justice. He was willing to struggle on behalf of the least powerful. But he carried on his dangerous battle for justice in a nonviolent mode that affirmed the humanity of his enemies and conferred dignity upon his followers. Is nonviolence then the answer to the dilemma created for Christians by the dual obligation to avoid harming and to protect the innocent? Is nonviolence incumbent upon all Christians as the exemplification of love which constitutes their distinctive contribution to the common life?

We can explore these ancient issues with the aid of a contemporary illustration centered upon events of tragic memory that raise perennial test questions which eventually emerge in every debate on the bounds of obligation to nonviolence. Examination of some hypothetical situations may help bare the reasoning employed in assessing the justifiable and unjustifiable uses of violence.

Suppose an officer of the Southern Christian Leadership Conference standing on the motel balcony in Memphis alongside Martin Luther King, Jr., the night he was shot in April, 1968, had seen the assassin lower his rifle in the window across the way. What should he have done? Whatever courses of conduct might be conjured up in retrospect, it seems most likely that any one of Dr. King's lieutenants would willingly have leaped in front of him so that he might live and their common cause prosper. At any rate, it is clear that such a man, having committed himself to nonviolence, would not have been armed and could not have fired a shot which would have preempted the attack.

What if a more ordinary Christian with no special ties to Dr. King had happened into the room where the assassin was poised? What should he have done? Should he retreat from danger and notoriety by withdrawing quickly and minding his own affairs? Or should he cast himself upon the would-be killer and risk his own life in the effort to spare another man? As a private citizen holding no special warrant from society, would it be justifiable for him to wound or to kill in the attempt to forestall murder?

There were many policemen in the vicinity of the motel. If one of them had seen the rifle aimed at Dr. King, should he have fired upon the assailant? Should an officer of the law, charged with responsibility for preserving peace and protecting peaceable citizens, abstain from doing violence in such circumstances?

Common opinion would doubtless expect and approve different forms of response from each of the three men in our test cases. To most it will seem reasonable to say that the three men have different callings, fill different offices, and may, in good conscience, behave in a manner appropriate for one who has assumed his particular office or station.

Dr. King and his followers have declared themselves to be advocates and practitioners of nonviolence. It would be morally incongruous for them to contradict by deeds the teaching that has endowed them with impressive moral stature. Their power as leaders is rooted in a moral credibility which demands integrity of preachment and practice. They have bound themselves by a promise not to kill, even in self-defense. Theirs is a promise that makes sense in light of the faith that unmerited suffering is a source of redemptive and reconciling power. Martyrdom confirms the moral coherence of their life and thought.

The policeman has also made a promise, a promise to risk his own life in defense of the life and property of other men. It would be unseemly for him to withdraw from the obligation to fulfill that commitment when the duty becomes dangerous or unpopular. Uneven or intermittent attention to duty, which would deny equal protection of the law to all men, would mark a moral deficiency. As a servant of the community the policeman must risk his life in defense of any who need protection from unjust attack. Sudden adherence to nonviolent ideals by a Memphis policeman in a position to avert the assassination would not have marked a triumph of high morality; it would have been a suspicious and serious derilection of duty.

Those who take nonviolence to be the norm of Christian behavior are obliged to question whether any Christian can, in good conscience, serve as a policeman, knowing that resort to violent means is a latent commitment of his office. If to be a Christian one must be nonviolent, then no Christian should assume the office of policeman, soldier, or magistrate. Christians should then pursue their high calling of nonviolence without assuming posts in which their scruples may endanger the potential victims of demented assassins. But then how is the obligation to protect the innocent and to vindicate justice to be fulfilled in a world of violent men? If Christians withdraw from public office, who will fill such posts and what norms will restrain the conduct of officials invested with powerful means of counterviolence? How may the policeman, the soldier, the magistrate know when it is and is not appropriate to employ restraining force if Christians shun the effort to elaborate a code to guide the behavior of those unable to affirm or practice the ideal of perfect nonviolence? What is the source of the ethic that should control their conduct? Do those who aspire to follow an ethic of saintliness bear an obligation to assist in the direct and explicit moral education of those of less heroic moral impulses?

If the disciples of nonviolence are morally bound not to use violence and the policeman is bound to use violence in certain circumstances but not in others, what of the ordinary Christian layman who, happening upon the scene of an intended assassination, may either assume or evade grave risk in preventing injustice? Should he intervene or pass by? We cannot, in short compass, do justice to the complexities of the moral reasoning that should determine his response. He must be concerned for the welfare of his neighbor the assassin as well as for his neighbor the victim. He must weigh the interests of the wider society and the specific concern his family may have for his own safety. He must ask whether there is any probably successful means of halting the murder short of attacking the attacker. If not, the logic of the dominant strand of Christian ethical thought places a heavy burden of proof upon those who would not risk their lives in the attempt to spare the victims of unjust attack.

Reflection upon our hypothetical cases leads to a distinction of different offices or callings, each with its own appropriate response to the act of a would-be assassin. Each office has its own form of expressing selflessness and concern for the neighbor. Each can entail both physical and spiritual dangers. There is an ethic appropriate for saints, for the practitioners of radical discipleship gathered together in an *ecclesiola in ecclesia,* or a small church within the church. There is a form of integrity appropriate for the ordinary Christian who prepares himself and those dependent upon him to respond bravely in an emergency which demands a difficult choice among neighbors who claim his love. There is also an integrity of the public officer willing to risk his life for the protection of all citizens equally and capable of discriminating between situations in which resort to violence is and is not justifiable.

Protestants have generally been uncomfortable with the suggestion that there may be different levels, grades, or modes of Christian discipleship. They have often tried to make one single ethic, one set of obligations govern the behavior of all believers, or, at times, even of all citizens. In choosing a single mode of discipleship as a norm for all men, Protestants have tended to convert the ethic of the saint into a rule for all men. This high ambition has been particularly evident in the history of America where sectarian piety has reinforced the Calvinistic commitment to transform the world. The transformation and renewal of the common life has been the historic vocation of the nation. America was envisioned as the harbinger of the Kingdom of God on earth, a kingdom in which violence would not disrupt a new order built upon moral concord.

American reality has been marked by violence. But the American dream has been a vision of nonviolence. The tremendous outpouring of grief and respect for Martin Luther King, Jr., from all segments of American society suggests that he was mourned not so much as a Christian martyr—a model of the piety inculcated by one church body within a religiously pluralistic society—but, rather, as a saint of the American civil religion. His nonviolent philosophy echoes an aspiration deeply woven into the implicit American civil creed. Long before Dr. King became active, Americans had indulged in crusades designed to banish war and abolish the use of force from history. To paraphrase Rap Brown, "In the realm of ideas, nonviolence is as American as cherry pie."

The aspiration to conform to the ethic of the saintly minority in both domestic and international affairs has been a long and strong thread in the fabric of American thought. When conduct has fallen short of the ethic of the saints, we have interpreted our violent acts as emergency measures, as acts out of character, analogous to those that might be taken by the ordinary Christian stumbling upon the assassin about to commit his deed. Once such emergencies were over, expectations reverted once again to the level of the ethic of the saints, an ethic that has been well defined, widely admired, but never implemented in public policy. Aspiration has soared. But when performance has sagged, there has been no strong, basic supporting ethical framework to prevent a thorough collapse. Thus, in the period between World Wars I and II pacifist enthusiasts heaped disdain upon the "sophistries" of the just war doctrine which might be used to justify some future resort to armed force. Categories necessary for discrimination between acceptable and unacceptable uses of violence were virtually expunged from the conscience of the public and its leadership. Thereafter, the "emergency measures" of World War II, including the obliteration bombing of civilian areas in Dresden, the fire bombing of Tokyo, and the atomic bombing of Hiroshima and Nagasaki, were not effectively challenged, let alone restrained by a public, which, ironically, had been inculcated with a crusading mentality by zealous and well-intentioned "crusaders for peace." Any crusade constitutes an invitation to habits of indiscriminating thought which erodes moral restraints. The charge that the just war doctrine has not effectively curbed national ambition and has been stretched to legitimate every regime's lust for dominion is a plausible criticism that becomes ironic when the restraining power of the just war doctrine is compared with that of alternative modes of reasoning concerning the morality of war. It would take a curious reading of history to suggest that the simpler logics of the crusade or pacifism have provided stronger restraints. These alternatives are reassuring in peacetime but lead to moral disaster in wartime. Those who adhere to the ethic of the saint must never, never indulge in war, for they will then have no habitual modes of moral discrimination to guard them from committing barbarities under the guise of their presumed virtuous intent. Those who are to be saints must not be saintly only part-time. Those who are called upon and from time to time accept the role of the policeman in their local communities or in the community of the world need to think critically about the ethic of the policeman. Seldom have American Christian scholars and laymen addressed themselves seriously to the task of helping public officers reflect upon the mode of reasoning appropriate to their office that would guide them in determining when they should act, how they should act, and why. They have given a great deal of advice upon specific issues but have been less assiduous in exposing the logic by which policy makers could derive morally commendable conclusions. The office of the policeman is not simply a temporary, embarrassing expedient. Those who hold the office deserve counsel and instruction. Too much has been left to individual intuition or to common sentiment highly vulnerable to momentary passions generated in crises. The implication has been that persistent moral instruction would be presumptuous and superfluous. If policemen, soldiers, and magistrates were "good men," it would be unnecessary; if they were "bad men," it would be useless. Given the currently widespread dissatisfaction with the performance of the role of the policeman by Americans at home and abroad, high priority should be assigned to the task of thinking through the moral criteria of proper conduct by those who occupy that office.

The just war theory provides an ethic for the policeman, the soldier, and the magistrate. It is a compromise, but a compromise which makes it possible to acknowledge both the claim of not harming and the obligation of protecting the innocent. It is grounded in a strong presumption against the use of violence, a presumption established for the Christian by the non-resistant example of Jesus and for the rational non-Christian by prudent concern for order and mutual security. This presumption against resort to violence may be overcome only by the necessity to vindicate justice and to protect the innocent against unjust aggressors. Hence, force must always be restrained because its only legitimate function is to restrain.

The logic of justifiable war works itself out into a number of criteria which define when an exception to the general ban against violence may be allowed and restraining force employed with tragic sorrow but still with good conscience. These criteria are rediscovered again and again by those who have pondered similar questions in earlier generations. The traditional doctrine of the just war, refined through centuries, is distinctive not in the questions it asks but in the degree of elaboration of the criteria it provides. Everyone who has inquired out of prudence, piety, or pity into the propriety of the use of force has constructed an analogue of "the just war doctrine." The merit of the version we have inherited rests in its high level of refinement achieved through continual testing against the entire range of human concerns in diverse circumstances. The just war doctrine is the precipitate of moral reflection upon political experience in the West. Its criteria provide an index to the moral economy underlying the use of force; they specify the types of actions that will eventually entail a high political and moral cost. Of all forms of thinking about the limits of justifiable use of force, the just war doctrine comes closest to providing relevant principles that are intelligible, generalizable, and capable of consistent application.

7

CHRISTIAN PARTICIPATION IN AN INTERNATIONAL POLICE FORCE

Observance of the canons of intelligibility, generalizability, and consistency are indispensable for the maintenance of the credibility and potency of moral protest against the evils of war. Those who debate the morality of the war in Vietnam bear an obligation to consider whether the reasons they advance for or against the war will be applicable in future situations. If Christians someday come to live under a worldwide public authority, it will still be necessary to inquire, in each new circumstance, whether resort to force is morally justifiable in its occasion and form. Reasons given today must be tested against tomorrow's circumstance. An appealing argument for immediate peace in Vietnam which, in the long run, could disallow actions necessary for the realization of a stable peace upheld throughout the world by international peace-keeping forces, should be subjected to rigorous criticism.

The vision of a worldwide public authority empowered to preserve peace performs a crucial function in very disparate styles of thought. For some crusaders the realization of such an authority is a cause worth fighting for. For many who label themselves pacifists, its present absence provides a reason for protesting rather than fighting. For most just war theorists, its possible evolution through application of well formed political judgment serves as an excuse for not protesting.

Acceptance of the just war criteria virtually demands affirmation of the desirability of an institutional embodiment of the common humanity of all mankind. Given even a mild sense of discrepancy between the criteria of the just war and current American military policy, the only logically and psychologically adequate means of abstaining from radical protest is to reaffirm vigorously the need for surrender of sovereignty to an effective international authority able to enforce the rule of law within a universal world community. The relevance of the just war theory, which seems to be belied by present military and political facts, is preserved by asserting that it renders a peculiarly profound insight regarding the occasion of war and the conditions which must be attained if peace is to be secure. Just wars occur when the bearer of a valid legal claim for redress of injury has, of necessity, to serve as his own judge and enforcer in the absence of an effective higher authority. As Grotius observed: "A just cause of war is injury done us, and nothing else . . . It is evident that there are as many sources for wars as there are for legal actions; then where no judgments are given war begins."[24] If wars are to be prevented, conscientious citizens and statesmen must seek to reduce the incidence of injury and to provide for redress of injury through means other than war. They must promote economic development and social stability through aid and technical assistance and also, through the gradual relinquishment of national sovereignty, help to construct a firm institutional context for the pacific settlement of disputes. Justice must be invoked and served not only in time of war; the just war doctrine established a persistent imperative for the establishment of a just society within which the bonds of common humanity will not be severed by aggression.

Christians who hold conflicting attitudes toward war may share the belief that some form of worldwide public authority is desirable. The effective source of disagreement concerning current questions of policy is discrepancy of judgment regarding the likeliest mode of transition to a new world order. But what will Christians of differing persuasions have to say after the transition has been made?

In order to carry out the task I have assigned to the ethicist, let us test the implications of various arguments in a hypothetical future situation in which a world government is struggling to be born. We will leap over the very perplexing problem of transition. Admittedly, the mode of its occurrence would have a significant effect upon the contours of issues in the new situation. But let us suppose that a world body has been able to recruit and finance a standing fighting force able to function without veto by one of the great powers. Under this new order, men are still animated by contentious spirits, are still prone to develop loyalties to lesser communities, and still possess memory of the skill to make weapons of mass destruction. A perfectly just distribution of goods and opportunities has not yet been achieved. In some quarters, rapid technological and social change brings upheaval and lags in adjustment; elsewhere, lack of change stimulates the ferment of frustration. The sense of common aspiration and the commitment to collective security is strong, but a completely stable and peaceful system has not been attained. Within the world community, neighbors still inflict and suffer injury. In order to insure proper recourse, international legislative and judicial institutions have been strengthened and the international armed force has been created to implement their decisions.[25] Under what circumstances could a Christian serve in that force? As a member of the force, engaged in the implementation of a sanction imposed by a duly constituted international tribunal, what acts may he, in good conscience, perform?

The recurrence of these two familiar questions under-lines the necessity of speaking not merely of Christian attitudes toward war and peace, but rather of Christian def-initions of the justifiable use of force. Should the engage-ment of an international force in combat incidental to the task of preserving peace in a region of continuing civil dis-cord such as Cyprus, Kashmir, northeast Thailand, Biafra, or along the west bank of the Jordan River be defined as war? No matter what term is applied, the action is liable to involve the taking of life, perhaps on a considerable scale. All Christians have an aversion to killing. Can they, neverthe-less, undertake to serve the cause of stability and peace by joining or supporting the international fighting force?

A thoroughgoing pacifist, bound by an absolute rejec-tion of killing under any and all circumstances, could not participate. But it seems that there are some who call them-selves pacifists who would bear arms in a peace-keeping venture under international authority. Their assumption of the title "pacifist" is logically odd. They apparently are not averse to killing in itself, but to killing under the wrong auspices or for an inappropriate cause or before the last peaceful resort has been exhausted or for selfish intentions. Our test case reveals that they are surreptitious users of a truncated version of the *jus ad bellum*. It is not incredible to suppose that, having despised or neglected study of the logic of justifiable use of force, they would be, once en-listed in a noble cause, vulnerable to the adoption of a cru-sading mentality. The *jus in bello* might have no power to restrain those now zealous in a worthy cause. What if the unjust aggressors, against whom the judgment of an interna-tional tribunal had been rendered by due process of law, became increasingly furious in their resistance, enlisted allies, and prepared to fight a civil war within the new world community? Mindful of the menace of a relapse into international anarchy, the noble cause of world government could not lightly be abandoned. With stakes so high, a very intense military effort could seem proportionate in the battle to make the world safe for humanity. If nuclear weapons were reinvented and brandished by the outlaw state, what should be the response of the international community? Would the dream of world rule of law be forsaken if judgments could not be enforced with the use only of discriminating weapons? Would bomb protestors march against the seat of world government?

The moral quandaries of the Christian will become more rather than less sharp if we come closer to an approximation of world government. The essence of such a new order must be the rule of law. The first necessity of any system of law is the maintenance of public order through an effective monopoly of force capable of preventing recourse to violence by lesser units. Under the rule of law, "war," or any extensive military action, would always be either a crime or a sanction imposed by the community against a crime.[26] There could be no neutrality or impartiality as the power under the jurisdiction of the world government evolves toward the status of an international police force. To kill a man in combat would be, for the Christian, either a grievous sin of murder or a tragic task of fortitude incumbent upon those serving as officers of the universal community.

A lack of fortitude would constitute a severe threat to hopes for a stable world order. A revealing passage in Grotius suggests that, throughout history, programs of collective security have failed and the power to make war has been left to the unfettered conscience of potential belligerents not only because of the difficulty of establishing agencies able to render objective judgments concerning the justice of the contending causes, but because men and nations are not readily induced to bear the risks of imposing the unpredictable sanction of violence.

> ... for other nations to offer to pronounce on the right of war between two peoples, would be dangerous for those who interfered, and who might thus be involved in a war belonging to others ... And in the next place, it can scarcely be known by external indications, in a just war, what is the proper limit of self-defense, of recovery of property, or of exaction of punishment; so that it is by all means better to leave this to the conscience of the belligerents, than to appeal to extraneous decision.[27]

Given the realities of the present system—continuing enmity between nations, instability within nations, and the prospect of the spread of nuclear weapons—few Christian commentators profess to believe that it is by all means better to leave the decision to go to war to the conscience of the belligerents. But who will forego whatever security and comfort they have achieved to run the risk of killing or being killed as a member of an international peace-keeping force? One is reminded of the story of the clever mice who realized that they could have peace and security by tying a bell around the neck of the marauding cat so they could be forewarned of its incursions. The plan came to naught when no one would volunteer in response to the inquiry, Now who among us has the courage to tie the bell around the neck of the cat? Undoubtedly, many mice who remained silent themselves later fell victim to the unfettered feline.

8
CONTINUING MORAL DILEMMAS

The evolution of an international police force would bring a crisis of conscience for adherents of each of the traditional Christian attitudes toward war and peace and a test of the intelligibility, generalizability, and consistency of their mode of reasoning. There would be a tendency toward polarization between the extremes of absolute pacifism and the crusade.

Refusal on principle to serve in the police force of an international community would be a more radical act than objection to induction into the armed services of a particular nation. Such action, it would seem, could be sustained only by an absolute refusal to be placed under the risk of killing another man. The charge of Celsus, that Christians are guilty of *contemptissima inertia* or most reprehensible sloth in their refusal to join in defense of the order that sustains the common life, would have renewed impact.

Nonabsolutist "pacifists" would find that many of their current arguments unwittingly grounded upon hidden appropriation of the criteria of the *jus ad bellum* would lose much of the appeal they have in a nationalistic setting. It would be more difficult to launch a moral deterrent to the use of an international police force by arguing that their action is illegal, futile, or selfish. Nonabsolutist pacifists would be required to clarify the bases of their objections to the use of violence. In so doing, they would have to move towards absolute pacifism or become explicit in their espousal of the criteria of justifiable use of force in company with just war theorists or, perchance, give evidence of their latent intellectual affinity for the crusading approach.

Just war theorists would also have thinking to do. Under a world state, the two perennial questions regarding the justifiable participation in the use of force would still recur in the pastoral as well as the political setting. Christians must reserve the right to inquire into the justice of the cause and the conduct of police actions. Their avowal of the *jus ad bellum,* which has provided a stimulus to the creation of an international system, could be a threat to the integrity of that system. For the justice of a cause may never come to be perfectly identified with its legality. A world government would not be elevated above the possibility of error and the temptation to tyranny. Only by surrendering the tradition of natural law and natural rights and accepting a Hobbesian positivistic view of justice could Christians remove the possibility that they might deem justice to be on the side of those condemned by due process and made the objects of armed repression. The dilemmas of selective conscientious objection, which we feel so keenly at this moment in the United States, would persist.[28] They are inherent in the tradition of the just war.

Christian convictions concerning the *jus in bello* add another dimension of difficulty. There is the possibility that a military action rightly begun with respect to the *jus ad bellum* cannot be pursued to victory without violation of the *jus in bello*. When that possibility is perceived, there is an obvious temptation to bend the criteria or to abandon them and adopt the stance of the crusader confronting barbarians and savages to whom civilized warriors owe no regard. This tendency to restrict the application of norms held to be intelligible, generalizable, and consistent, raises piercing questions concerning the validity of the specific criteria thus challenged, the utility of the just war doctrine itself, and eventually, the role of principles of moral thought and the limits of moral discourse.

There is not presently available a mode of reasoning concerning the justifiable use or nonuse of force that is capable of rendering solutions to our present moral dilemmas. These dilemmas will not disappear even if a new world order appears. What are the theological and ethical implications of this impasse? We must induce theologians to reflect upon what God is doing in leaving us perplexed and vulnerable to our own freedom to destroy our global history. As ethicists, we must, in turn, give highest priority to careful reconsideration of the limits and functions of various modes of moral discourse in different contexts, lest we be left to the play of capricious whim or the definition of "right" as the will of the strongest.

9

AN
ANTICIPATED
RECAPITULATION

We can theorize that if we are ever to reach the level of world government we have posited, it will be only after striking recapitulation in coming years of the history of the first thousand years of Christian thought on Christian participation in the use of force. An outburst of quasi-pacifist sentiment might help sensitize men anew to the inhumanity of war and generate an imperative to change. But in the moral and political realm there is danger of pacifist overkill. Unless one can believe in the sudden metamorphosis of man, the control of violence must be reckoned to be a continuing problem. Into the distant future it will be necessary to observe that "the most difficult problem which today confronts world public order is that of characterizing and preventing unlawful violence."[29] In order to make the distinctions between justifiable and unjustifiable forms of violence which are indispensable to the creation of a legal order, men will have to retrieve or reinvent criteria approximating those transmitted through the just war tradition. A moral summons will be issued for citizens to assume responsibility for the vindication of justice. The words may be those modeled by Ambrose upon the text of Cicero: *"Qui non repellit a socio injuriam, si potest, tam est in vitio quam ille qui fecit"*[30] "For he who does not ward off injury from a comrade, when

he is able to, is just as guilty as he who does the injury."
Christians will be called upon to share the task of realizing
the new order they have envisioned by joining in a crusade
against its enemies. They may hear from the lips of the
secretary-general of the beleaguered world body a call to
a crusade sounding like a secularized echo of the exhortation
delivered by Pope Gregory VII in the eleventh century:

> . . . the example of our Redeemer and the duty of fraternal
> charity urges us to lay down our lives for the freedom of our
> brethren: for as He laid down His life for us, so we also ought
> to lay down our lives for our brethren. Know therefore that,
> confiding in the mercy of God and in the power of His virtue,
> we are doing and preparing all things that we may speedily
> and with God's help succour the Christian Empire. We beg
> you therefore by the faith in which you are united in the
> adoption of the sons of God, and we admonish you by the
> authority of St. Peter, prince of the Apostles, to be moved to
> compassion by the wounds and blood of the brethren and the
> peril of the aforesaid empire, that your virtue may, for Christ's
> sake, willingly take up the cause and bring help to the
> brethren.[31]

Once unleashed, crusading zeal is difficult to restrain.
The faithful may be reminded that they have an obligation
not only to protect the innocent from the depredation of
unjust aggressors but to protect the wicked from themselves.
Augustine laid a foundation for such a high-minded crusade:

> . . . it is not innocent to spare a man at the risk of his falling
> into graver sin. To be innocent, we must not only do harm to
> no man, but also restrain him from sin or punish his sin, so that
> either the man himself who is punished may profit by his ex-
> perience, or others be warned by his example.[32]

We have a duty to seek the welfare of all our neighbors.
Their welfare requires public order. Even if we, like Augustine, forego the right of private self-defense,[33] we must be
concerned for the defense of public peace and justice. But

how far can we go in exercising defense? The central question is embedded in Augustine's affirmation that as long as the City of God and the earthly city "are commingled, we also enjoy the peace of Babylon."

> Even the heavenly city, therefore, while in its state of pilgrimage, avails itself of the peace of earth, and, so far as it can without injuring faith and godliness, desires and maintains a common agreement among men regarding the acquisition of the necessaries of life, and makes this earthly peace bear upon the peace of heaven ...[34]

As a citizen of a new world order empowered with an international police force, what acts may I commit or support in the service of our common peace "without injuring faith and godliness"? Does godliness require that killing be absolutely forbidden to Christians? Or does faith command that the direct, intentional killing of the innocent be absolutely forbidden? Is godliness compatible with the idea that killing is justified whenever it is a necessary means for preserving a stable world government? The distinctions of the pacifist, the just war theorist, and the crusader will be carried over into the new day in which decisions must be made concerning the use of force in the service of a world polity.

We have traveled a long way to arrive at "the same old questions." But it will be useful if it provides an antidote to the easy appeal to the future to evade or to ease the dilemmas of the present. We may or may not achieve some form of world government. But there will be no new order in which we will be spared moral agony and the travail of conscience. I take this to be the underlying message of Book Nineteen of the *City of God*, the setting in which Augustine deals most explicitly with the question of war. The Book is a critique of the ethical thought of secular philosophers and all those who "have, with a marvellous shallowness, sought to find their blessedness in this life and in themselves."[35] Clearly, our supreme good cannot be in this life, for "what flood of eloquence can suffice to detail the miseries of this life?"[36] ". . . who can enumerate all the great grievances with which human society abounds in the misery of this mortal state?"[37] ". . . the actual possession of the happiness of this life, without the hope of what is beyond, is but a false happiness and profound misery. For the true blessings of the soul are not now enjoyed . . ."[38] In this life, virtue must wage a perpetual war with vices. War is the theme of Book Nineteen—war within the self, within the family, within the city and the empire, and finally, hell is war. One can ask, says Augustine, "what it is in war that is hurtful and destructive, and he shall see that it is nothing else than the mutual opposition and conflict of things."[39] This conflict is rooted in the disordered quality of man's existence apart from God. Even if we were to succeed in evangelizing the world in this generation, conflicts originating in divided wills would not cease upon the earth. Christian ethicists should report to men that this is so and assist them in the task of restraining by moral suasion and by law the passions they cannot control by a simple act of will.

This Augustinian epilogue will be discouraging to those who have placed undue hopes upon the realization of peace and justice in this world. Concerted reflection upon the ambiguities of using or not using force and upon the possibility that men armed with nuclear weapons may foreclose their future upon this earth can lead only to the conclusion that the ultimate fulfillment of the promises of a God faithful to his covenant is not dependent upon the continuation of our sojourn upon this planet. The Christian who knows that "the peace which is peculiar to ourselves we enjoy now with God by faith, and shall hereafter enjoy eternally with Him by sight"[40] is set free to labor with calm strength for the penultimate good which is the peace of the earthly city.

Augustine reminds us that the uncertain peace of earthly kingdoms "is not to be lightly esteemed."[41] But the severe dilemma from which we will not soon escape is expressed in Augustine's observation, "It is . . . with the desire for peace that wars are waged . . ."[42] This is the tragic dimension of human life reflected in the *locus classicus* of the just war doctrine.

> But, say they, the wise man will wage just wars. As if he would not all the rather lament the necessity of just wars, if he remembers that he is a man; for if they were not just he would not wage them, and would therefore be delivered from all wars. For it is the wrong-doing of the opposing party which compels the wise man to wage just wars; and this wrong-doing, even though it gave rise to no war, would still be matter of grief to man because it is man's wrong-doing. Let every one, then, who thinks with pain on all these great evils, so horrible, so ruthless, acknowledge that this is misery. And if any one either endures or thinks of them without mental pain, this is a more miserable plight still, for he thinks himself happy because he has lost human feeling.[43]

Augustine conceded the tragic necessity that would compel the policeman, the soldier, the magistrate to have recourse to violent means to repel an unjust aggressor. But he did not lose sight of the high calling of the saint or overlook the happier vocation of the Christian peacemaker. He wrote to Darius, a court official of Valentinian III sent to North Africa in 429 to avert a war with the Vandals:

> But the truly great and those who have their own glory are not only the bravest warriors but the most faithful—and this is a source of truer praise. These are the men by whose toils and perils, with the help of God's protection and support, an invincible foe is subjugated, peace is won for the state as well as for the provinces, restored to order. But it is a greater glory to destroy war with a word than men with a sword, and to secure and maintain peace by means of peace rather than by

war. There is no doubt that those who fight are also seeking peace, if they are good men, but they are seeking it through bloodshed, whereas you have been sent to prevent blood from being shed. On others rests the necessity of killing; on you, the blessedness of forestalling the taking of life. Therefore . . . rejoice in that great and true blessing which is yours, and enjoy it in God to whom you owe it that you are such a man and that you are undertaking such a worthy task.[44]

On those who seek justice day by day rests the blessedness of forestalling the taking of life.

NOTES

1. Paul Ramsey has written on *War and the Christian Conscience* (Durham, N.C.: Duke University Press, 1961). Edward LeRoy Long, Jr., has contributed a volume on *War and Conscience in America* (Philadelphia: The Westminster Press, 1968). John Coleman Bennett edited a symposium on *Nuclear Weapons and the Conflict of Conscience* (New York: Charles Scribner's Sons, 1962). *Nuclear Weapons and Christian Conscience* (London: Merlin Press, 1961) contains a series of essays by British Roman Catholic nuclear pacifists. Peter Mayer has edited an anthology entitled *The Pacifist Conscience* (New York: Holt, Rinehart and Winston, 1966). For a more extended list of relevant materials see the bibliographical essay.

2. Paul Lehmann, the foremost expositor of contextual ethics among serious theologians, perceives that his position is not a promising basis for public discourse on matters of common concern in a pluralistic society. "The crucial problem of Christian ethics in the context of the *koinonia* is how the behavior of Christians is to be related to the behavior of non-Christians. How can a *koinonia* ethic make any ethical claims upon those in society who do not acknowledge the *koinonia* as their point of departure and frankly live neither in it nor by its light? Do we have here a kind of double ethical standard: one for Christians and another for non-Christians?" *Ethics in a Christian Context* (New York: Harper & Row, Publishers, 1963), p. 145. Lehmann rejects the natural law tradition as "ethically inadequate both in itself and as a possibility open to a *koinonia* ethic"

(p. 148). But, noting the penchant for illustrations drawn from simpler, dyadic relationships and the inconclusiveness of Lehmann's discussion of the problem of the Christian's relationship to war (pp. 140-145), a reader interested in public affairs may conclude that, with the tools left at his disposal, Lehmann is not able to discuss issues of public policy in a manner likely to be recognized as helpful beyond a circle of theologically attuned Christians. His response to the critical problem he has raised is to note that "A *koinonia* ethic may thus conceivably dispose of the problem of a double standard by including the unbelievers among the other sheep of the Holy Spirit of God" (p. 159). This solution has the merit of leaving all men reliant upon the Spirit that "bloweth where it listeth" (John 3:8, K.J.V.) and equally uncertain regarding right and wrong in war.

3. The four categories correspond generally to Parsons' "patterns of empirical existential ideas," "patterns of expressive symbolization," "patterns of evaluation," and "patterns of the grounding of meaning," which the true initiate will recognize as the "adaptive," "goal attainment," "integrative," and "latent pattern of maintenance" boxes of the cultural subsystem of the general theory of action. See especially, Talcott Parsons, "Culture and the Social System: Introduction," in *Theories of Society: Foundations of Modern Sociological Theory*, Talcott Parsons, Edward Shils, Kaspar D. Naegele, and Jesse R. Pitts, editors (New York: The Free Press of Glencoe, 1961), Vol. 2, Pt. 4, pp. 963-993. An extravagant elaboration of the analytical paradigm adapted from Parsons' theory appears in Ralph B. Potter, "The Structure of Certain American Christian Responses to the Nuclear Dilemma, 1958-1963," unpublished doctoral dissertation, Harvard Divinity School, 1965.

4. See Henry David Aiken, *Reason and Conduct: New Bearings in Moral Philosophy* (New York: Alfred A. Knopf, 1962), Ch. 4, "Levels of Moral Discourse," pp. 65-87.

5. See George C. Kerner, *The Revolution in Ethical Theory* (Oxford: The Clarendon Press, 1966), especially pp. 209-212.

6. Many of the essays of Paul Ramsey dealing with the morality of war are gathered in the volume *The Just War* (New York: Charles Scribner's Sons, 1968).

7. Much more thorough discussions of the requirements of moral argument may be found in the professional writings of philosophical ethicists. See, for example, John Rawls, "Outline of a Decision Procedure for Ethics," *Philosophical Review*, Vol. 60 (1951), pp. 177-97 and "Justice as Fairness," *Philosophical Review*, Vol. 62 (1958), pp. 164-94, reprinted in *Justice and Social Policy: A Collection of Essays*, edited, with an introduction by Frederick A. Olafson (Englewood Cliffs, N.J.: Prentice-Hall, Inc., 1961); also, Roderick Firth, "Ethical Absolutism and the Ideal Observer Theory," *Philosophy and Phenomenological Research*, Vol. 12 (1952), pp. 317-345. Richard A. Brandt, *Ethical Theory: The Problems of Normative and Critical Ethics* (Englewood Cliffs, N.J.: Prentice-Hall, Inc., 1959) provides a reliable introduction to the field of philosophical ethics and extensive bibliographical clues. A briefer survey is available in William K. Frankena, *Ethics* (Englewood Cliffs, N.J.: Prentice-Hall, 1963). A portion of Frankena's work provided the basis for the major distinctions of Paul Ramsey's volume, *Deeds and Rules in Christian Ethics* (New York: Charles Scribner's Sons, 1967).

8. See Brandt, *op. cit.*, Ch. 2: "Two Tests of Ethical Principles: Consistency and Generality," pp. 16-36.

9. Marcus G. Singer, "Generalization in Ethics," *Mind*, Vol. 64 (1955), pp. 364, 371.

10. Henry Sidgwick, *The Methods of Ethics* (New York: Dover Publications, 1966), based on seventh edition, originally published 1907, p. 380.

11. Joseph Fletcher is the most popular exponent of situation ethics. His major exposition, *Situation Ethics: The New Morality* (Philadelphia: The Westminster Press, 1966), barely mentions the problem of war. Fletcher criticizes "classical pacifism" which "holds the use of violence to be always wrong regardless of the situation" as a form of legalism (p. 83). In a chapter devoted to the theme that love and justice are the same, he alludes to "the need for *a loving use of force* to protect the innocent and to make 'rights' practicable" (p. 100) and indicates that love may require civil disobedience or revolution (p. 101). "We ought not to hesitate to break a law that is in all conscience unjust, that is to say, unloving" (p. 101). Concerning the definition of legitimate occasions for the use of violence or the

morally defensible limits in the application of violence, it seems that for Fletcher "Every man must decide for himself according to his own estimates of conditions and consequences; and no one can decide for him or impugn the decision to which he comes" (p. 37). Victims of atrocities in war would appear to have little basis upon which to quibble with well-intentioned attackers.

12. The introductory note of a volume commissioned and published in January, 1968, by Clergy and Laymen Concerned About Vietnam reflects this pattern of reasoning: *In the Name of America:* "The conduct of the War in Vietnam by the armed forces of the United States as shown by published reports Compared with the Laws of War Binding on the United States Government and on its Citizens."

13. See, for example, Ian Brownlie, *International Law and the Use of Force by States* (New York: Oxford University Press, 1963), Ch. 8, "Criminal Responsibility for the Unlawful Use of Force in Inter-state Relations." Relevant bibliography is cited in footnote 1, p. 150.

14. See Ralph Potter, "Just War and Reasons of State," in *Just War and Vatican Council II: A Critique*, by Robert W. Tucker, with Commentary by George G. Higgins, Ralph Potter, Richard H. Cox, Paul Ramsey (New York: The Council on Religion and International Affairs, 1966), p. 58.

15. Otto A. Bird, *The Idea of Justice* (New York: Frederick A. Praeger, 1967), p. 164 *et passim.*

16. For texts tracing the development of Western thought concerning the criteria of a justifiable war, see the bibliographical note, pages 87-95.

17. Roland H. Bainton, *Christian Attitudes Toward War and Peace: A Historical Survey and Critical Re-evaluation* (New York: Abingdon Press, 1960), p. 14.

18. William V. O'Brien argues, for instance, that "it may be questioned whether non-combatant immunity as an absolute principle is compatible with the exercise of the legitimate rights of defense which Catholic social teaching has so often and so recently reiterated . . . But the Church, well aware of the character of modern war, has confirmed the continued

existence of the right of defense. We are left, therefore, with the question whether the good of saving one's society through legitimate defense is in some circumstances sufficient reason for the killing of non-combatants which must inevitably accompany such defense." *Nuclear War, Deterrence and Morality* (Westminster, Md.: Newman Press, 1966), pp. 83 f.

19. See *Nuclear Weapons and Christian Conscience,* edited by Walter Stein (London: Merlin Press, 1961).

20. See C. A. Pompe, *Aggressive War: An International Crime* (The Hague: Martinus Nijhoff, 1953), p. 126.

21. Myres S. McDougal and Florentine P. Feliciano, *Law and Minimum World Public Order: The Legal Regulation of International Coercion* (New Haven: Yale University Press, 1961): "In the theory and practice of international law during the nineteenth and early twentieth centuries, *bellum iustum* had for all practical purposes been brought to an unobtrusive demise. Resort to coercion was, in the view of most publicists and state officials . . . the exercise of an attribute or prerogative of sovereignty, the legitimacy of which nonparticipating states were not competent to judge. Traditional international law included no prescription for controlling a resort to coercion or for characterizing coercion as permissible or non-permissible; it attempted only the regulation and humanization of violence once violence had in fact been initiated. In theory, the contending belligerents stood on a plane of 'juridical equality,' and third states which chose not to participate were said to be under a 'duty of impartiality' and nondiscrimination in their relations with both belligerents . . . (a) deep internal contradiction in the structure of world prescriptions developed: the right to independent existence, though classed as a fundamental right of states, did not include a prohibition against states waging war and destroying one another. The international law of the nineteenth century may thus be seen to represent a policy of indifference, as it were, to the common interest in restraining violence, and hence of permitting the speedy resolution of controversies between states simply on the basis of their relative strength. Its principal effort appeared to be to limit the spatial extension of violence through application of its 'neutrality' rules, designed in theory to isolate the contending belligerents and

practically tending to make superior indigenous strength decisive" (pp. 135 f.). "The most basic premise of the whole structure of prescription and doctrine was that recourse to violence
was an exercise of the discretionary competence of a sovereign
state and that other states were not entitled to sit in judgment
upon the legitimacy of either belligerent's cause" (p. 68).

22. See Robert W. Tucker, *The Just War: A Study in Contemporary American Doctrine* (Baltimore: The Johns Hopkins
Press, 1960): "The American doctrine is distinguished by the
assumption that the use of force is clearly governed by uni-
versally valid moral and legal standards; it is distinguished further by the insistence with which these standards are interpreted
as making the justice or injustice of war primarily dependent
upon the circumstances immediately attending the initiation of
force. In substance, the just war is the war fought either in self-
defense or in collective defense against an armed attack" (p. 11).

23. There are many subspecies of pacifism. All types of pacifists
are linked together here, *a la* Bainton, as upholders of a fundamental orientation to the problem of war which is inwardly
diverse but, nevertheless, distinguishable from belief in the crusade or the just war theory.

24. Hugo Grotius, *De Jure Belli et Pacis,* William Whewell,
editor and translator (Cambridge: John W. Parker, London,
1853), Vol. I, Lib. II, I, 4, p. 204. Translation revised.

25. For discussion of the prospects of such a force see Lincoln
P. Bloomfield, *et alia, International Military Forces: The Question of Peacekeeping in an Armed and Disarming World* (Boston: Little, Brown and Company, 1964).

26. See Hans Kelsen, *General Theory of Law and State* (New
York: Russell and Russell, 1961), pp. 328-341.

27. Grotius, *op. cit.,* Vol. III, Lib. III, IV, pp. 74 f.

28. See Ralph Potter, "Conscientious Objection to Particular
War," in *Religion and the Public Order,* Vol. 4, Donald Giannella, editor (Ithaca, N.Y.: Cornell University Press, 1968).

29. McDougal and Feliciano, *op. cit.,* p. 59.

30. Ambrose, *De Officiis Ministrorum,* I, 26. Compare, Cicero,
De Officiis, I, 23. Cited in John Eppstein, *The Catholic Tradition*

of the Law of Nations (London: Burns, Oates and Washbourne, Ltd., 1935), pp. 59 ff.

31. Gregory VII, Epistle XLIX, *Patrologiae Latina,* 148, Column 329, quoted in Eppstein, *op. cit.,* p. 94.

32. Augustine, *The City of God,* XIX: 16, translated by Marcus Dods (New York: The Modern Library, 1950), p. 695.

33. Augustine, Epistle 47: "In regard to killing men so as not to be killed by them, this view does not please me, unless perhaps it should be a soldier or a public official. In this case, he does not do it for his own sake, but for others or for the state to which he belongs, having received the power lawfully in accord with his public character." *The Fathers of the Church: Saint Augustine—Letters,* Vol. 1, translated by Wilfrid Parsons (New York: Fathers of the Church, Inc., 1951), p. 230. For comment upon a passage in *Augustine: Earlier Writings,* The Library of Christian Classics, Vol. 6, translated by John H. S. Burleigh (Philadelphia: The Westminster Press, 1953), Book I, v, 11, see Herbert A. Deane, *The Political and Social Ideas of St. Augustine* (New York: Columbia University Press, 1963), Ch. 5, footnote 22, pp. 311 f.

34. Augustine, *The City of God,* XIX: 17, p. 696.

35. *Ibid.,* XIX: 4, p. 676.

36. *Ibid.*

37. *Ibid.,* XIX: 5, p. 681.

38. *Ibid.,* XIX: 20, pp. 698 f.

39. *Ibid.,* XIX: 28, p. 709.

40. *Ibid,* XIX: 27, p. 707.

41. *Ibid.,* XIX: 26, p. 707.

42. *Ibid.,* XIX: 12, p. 687.

43. *Ibid.,* XIX: 7, pp. 683 f.

44. Augustine, Epistle 229, *The Fathers of the Church: Saint Augustine—Letters,* Vol. 5 (1956), pp. 152 f.

BIBLIOGRAPHICAL ESSAY

War has been a major institution throughout history. Its causes, conduct, and cures are treated in an immense literature. Less extensive is the literature devoted specifically to assessing or reforming the modes of thought by which men determine the rightness or wrongness of war. In sorting through the literature, I have tried to select materials which will be helpful in considering the question, How ought we to proceed in thinking about what is right and wrong in the initiation and conduct of war?

I must confess that in some of the longer works drawn from other disciplines I have read only those portions most directly relevant to historical and critical study in the field of ethics. I am very conscious of the severe dangers of intruding into neighboring disciplines. I am not competent to assess the contribution made, for example, by C. A. Pompe to the field of international law. I can, however, testify that his chapter "Evolution Toward Nuremberg" in *Aggressive War: An International Crime* (The Hague: Martinus Nijhoff, 1953) has been helpful to me as an ethicist intent upon understanding the common tradition of thought concerning justifiable and unjustifiable uses of violence. This review is necessarily an interim report upon materials that may be helpful to others as they have been to me in thinking about the questions treated in the preceding essay. I hope that it provides clues that will enable others to render these materials obsolete through the production of more precise and insightful analyses. I apologize for certain gaps and for the failure always to perceive and refer to the most definitive and up-to-date work on a given topic. Hopefully, an alert reader who attends to the footnotes and bibliographies provided in the volumes cited here, will be drawn on to further explorations in the field and will discover bibliographical treasures I have not unearthed.

For most people, the best place to begin is with Roland H. Bainton's *Christian Attitudes Toward War and Peace: A Historical Survey and Critical Re-evaluation* (New York: Abingdon Press, 1960). Bainton's survey is lucid, reliable, well documented, and available in paperback. The author treats the major figures and outlines the perennial issues in a manner which conveys a sense of the historical continuity of puzzlement and concern about the circumstances in which resort to force may be morally permissible. Bainton examines the thought of classical antiquity and provides a memorable typology which sorts Christian attitudes toward war into the three major categories of pacifism, the just war theory, and the crusade. His analysis provides an orderly framework, a map or guide, useful in further exploration. Extensive footnotes, citing an abundance of European literature, point to many paths of study. A much less adequate survey is presented in relatively brief, paperback form in *Christianity Versus Violence: A Social and Historical Study of War and Christianity*, by Stanley Windass (London: Sheed and Ward, 1964). Edward LeRoy Long, Jr., has published a popular review of the major positions which constitute current options in his paperback, *War and Conscience in America* (Philadelphia: The Westminster Press, 1968). Long separates "agonized participants in war" from crusaders and proponents of the just war doctrine and distinguishes three types of religious opposition to participation in war—"vocational," "activistic," and "transmoral" pacifism.

The tradition surveyed in such an orderly manner by Bainton has been treated in a more piecemeal fashion by other scholars. *The Catholic Tradition of the Law of Nations* by John Eppstein (London: Burns, Oates and Washbourne, Ltd., 1935) brings together extracts from documents not easily obtained elsewhere. It is a useful source book but, in neglecting the development of pacifist thought, it is less comprehensive or balanced than Bainton's volume. Eppstein and others have benefited from the diligence of Alfred Vanderpol who scoured traditional sources in compiling three significant works, the most famous of which is the posthumously published volume, *La doctrine scholastique du droit de guerre . . . avec une biographie de l'auteur* (by Emile Schemon) (Paris: A. Pedone, 1919). Vanderpol's earlier works were *La guerre devant le christianisme* (3rd ed., Paris: A. Tratin, 1911) and *Droit de guerre d'après les Theologiens et les Canonistes du Moyen Age* (Paris: A. Tratin, 1911).

Robert Regout intended his work, *La Doctrine de la guerre juste de Saint Augustin à nos jours d'après les Theologiens et les Canonistes Catholiques* (Paris: A. Pedone, 1935) to serve as a corrective to Vanderpol's emphases upon discontinuity in the development of the just war doctrine. Regout concludes that "the theory of the canonists and theologians concerning the legitimacy of war presents, from Saint Augustine to our own day, a coherent ensemble of fundamental ideas, the development of which is accomplished without interruption through the centuries" (p. 303, my translation). "Before as well as after Vitoria (d. 1546) writers consider that war is just only if it is absolutely necessary for the *defense* of rights against attack, for the *restoration* of rights when an injury has been sustained, for the *vindication* of violated justice. Each one of these causes taken separately is considered a sufficient justification of war, provided, naturally, that the other required conditions are satisfied" (p. 299, my translation).

Ernest Nys, in his volume, *Le droit de la guerre et les precurseurs de Grotius* (Paris: Durand et Pedone-Lauriel, 1882), notes that "prior to Grotius, the history of international law is limited to the history of the law of war, as the law of war exhausts all the material of international law" (p. 7). The law of war "forms the nucleus of international law." In exploring the history of their own discipline, students of international law have contributed to the clarification of the moral tradition. Nys claims that "it is not profitable to go back as far as antiquity; it did not have the notion of laws governing the relations among peoples" (p. 6). The two-volume work of Coleman Phillipson, however, provides an immense amount of information on how recurring problems of war and peace were dealt with in theory and practice. Excellent bibliography and annotation are given in Phillipson's volumes on *The International Law and Custom of Ancient Greece and Rome* (London: Macmillan and Company, Ltd., 1911). Extensive references to works dealing with issues that lie upon the boundary of international law and ethical analysis is also provided in *International Law and the Use of Force by States,* by Ian Brownlie (New York: Oxford University Press, Inc., 1963). In J. L. Brierly's book, *The Law of Nations: An Introduction to the International Law of Peace* (New York: Oxford University Press, Inc., 1963), the opening chapter on "The Origins of International Law" is an elaboration of the observation of Sir Henry Maine that "the grandest function of the law of nature was discharged in giving birth to modern international law." The development of the *jus ad bellum* is traced in the dissertation of William B. Ballis, published under the title, *The Legal*

Position of War: Changes in Its Practice and Theory from Plato to Vattel (The Hague: Martinus Nijhoff, 1937). Many of the most important primary sources have been republished by the Carnegie Endowment for International Peace in a series of Classics of International Law.

C. A. Pompe has contributed an extremely useful summary of the development of the just war doctrine and the concept of international penal law in his chapter, "Evolution Towards Nuremberg," in *Aggressive War: An International Crime*. The frequently cited work by Hans Wehberg, *The Outlawry of War* (Washington: Carnegie Endowment for International Peace, 1931) is considerably less helpful.

Forbidding in size but readable in content is the massive volume of Myres S. McDougal and Florentino P. Feliciano, *Law and Minimum World Public Order: The Legal Regulation of International Coercion* (New Haven: Yale University Press, 1961). Acquaintance with such works should induce a degree of humility in moralists who habitually evade the thorny details of specific choices which lawyers cannot circumvent with global evaluations.

Much helpful material can be found in law journals, which, happily, are very well indexed. In the article "Les droits de la juste victoire selon la tradition des theologiens catholiques," in *Revue Generale de Droit International Public*, XXXII (Tome VII, 2ème Serie, 1925), pp. 366-387, P. Yves de la Biere brings the tradition to bear upon questions concerning war guilt, reparations, and related issues. In a later article in the same journal, "Les etapes de la tradition theologique concernat le droit de la guerre juste: Notes d'Histoire des Doctrine," *Revue Generale de Droit International Public*, XLIV (3ème Serie, Tome XI, 1937), 129-161, de la Briere outlines the development of the just war doctrine and offers a helpful note on the life and work of

Alfred Vanderpol, expressing appreciation while suggesting necessary corrections (pp. 156-158). Other sketches of the history of the just war doctrine appear in Joachim von Elbe, "The Evolution of the Concept of the Just War in International Law," *American Journal of International Law,* Vol. 33, No. 4 (October, 1939), pp. 665-688, and Arthur Nussbaum, "Just War—A Legal Concept?" *Michigan Law Review,* Vol. 42, No. 3 (December, 1943) pp. 453-479. Nussbaum's doubts concerning the legal relevance of the just war theory are stated sharply by Josef L. Kunz in "Bellum Justum and Bellum Legale: Editorial Comment," *American Journal of International Law,* Vol. 45, No. 3 (July, 1951), pp. 528-534. Kunz views the traditional doctrine as an answer to the theological question, How can a Christian participate in war without incurring sin? The doctrine is impossible of legal implementation because it offers no objective criteria of injustice, does not overcome the problem of who is to decide, and fails to escape the difficulty that war is not an adequate means of enforcing judgments regarding justice, since the unjust side might prevail. Kunz sees the just war doctrine as undertaking the double function of enforcing both law and justice; he emphasizes that law and justice need not necessarily rest with the same party. In the twentieth century, according to Kunz, the establishment of the League of Nations, the Kellogg Pact, and the United Nations Charter do not represent a return to the traditional doctrine of the just war but its replacement with the concept of *bellum legale* rather than *bellum justum.* Kunz himself argued strenuously for the refurbishment of the laws of war in his article, "The Chaotic Status of the Laws of War and the Urgent Necessity for Their Revision," *American Journal of International Law,* Vol. 45, No. 1 (January, 1951), pp. 37-61.

Scholarly journals in disciplines other than the law may

also publish relevant articles such as "A Just War Analysis of Two Types of Deterrence," by Theodore Roszak, *Ethics*, Vol. 73, No. 2 (January, 1963), pp. 100-109; "Pacifism: A Philosophical Analysis," by Jan Narveson, *Ethics*, Vol. 75 (July, 1965), pp. 259-271; and "Ethics and War: A Catholic View," by Joseph C. McKenna, *The American Political Science Review*, Vol. 54, No. 3 (September, 1960), pp. 647-658.

There is a large amount of relevant literature compiled by political scientists whose concerns touch those of the ethicist at many points. Of special interest are *The Just War: A Study in Contemporary American Doctrine*, by Robert W. Tucker (Baltimore: The Johns Hopkins Press, 1960); *The State of War: Essays in the Theory and Practice of International Politics*, by Stanley Hoffman (New York: Frederick A. Praeger, 1965); and *Man, the State and War: A Theoretical Analysis* by Kenneth N. Waltz (New York: Columbia University Press, 1959). Waltz attempts to ascertain whether authors locate the causes of war within *man himself*, within the nature of the *domestic regime* in power in particular states, or within the *structure of the international context* in which states must exist. If the cause of war is located within man himself, within human nature, the remedy must be to change that nature through the infusion of grace, the processes of education, or whatever other means may be available. If the causes of war are traced to factors pertaining to the internal structure of states, such as a totalitarian political regime, economic destitution, or demographic pressure, the remedy for war would appropriately be sought through constitutional, economic reforms or through a program of limiting population expansion. If the anarchic structure of the international milieu is responsible for the frequent outbreaks of warfare, recourse must be had to the development of some broader form of political organization that will establish a monopoly of force. Waltz summarizes his central insight:

"Yet each attempt to alleviate a condition implies some idea of its cause: To explain how peace can be more readily achieved requires an understanding of the causes of war" (p. 2). *Plans for World Peace Through Six Centuries* are surveyed in a book with that descriptive title by Sylvester John Hemleben (Chicago: The University of Chicago Press, 1943).

I cannot vouch for the range of anthropological literature concerning the use and control of violence in primitive societies, some of which has been brought together in *Law and Warfare: Studies in the Anthropology of Conflict,* edited by Paul Bohannan, American Museum Sourcebooks in Anthropology (Garden City, N. Y.: The Natural History Press, 1967). In *The Law of War and Peace in Islam: A Study in Muslim International Law* (London: Luzac and Company, 1940), Majid Khadduri traces the development of the *Jihad,* which literally means "exertion," but took on the juridical-religious meaning of "the exertion of one's power in 'the path of *Allah,*' i.e., for the spread of the belief in *Allah* and that his *word* shall be supreme over the world" (p. 29). "In more precise and technical language the *Jihad* may be stated as a doctrine of permanent war . . . it is a state of war against the unbelievers until the whole world would be *islamized*" (p. 30 f.). Even though powerful religious emotions motivate the *Jihad,* it is not to be initiated and conducted without careful discrimination. Distinctions are made between justifiable and unjustifiable causes of war (p. 35). A *jus ad bellum* controls the occasion and initiation of war. "The custom was developed that fighting should be preceded by an 'invitation to Islam' and only failure to accept the new faith, or pay the tribute, would precipitate fighting with the enemy" (p. 47). Negotiations were to be pursued whenever they might forestall resort to battle. A *jus in bello* prescribed obligations with respect to persons and property in war.

The interests of students of Christian thought concerning the morality of war converge at many points not only with the concerns of scholars in world religions, international law, philosophical ethics, and political science, but also with pursuits of historians. There are innumerable studies of particular periods or movements which contain materials that could be employed in inductive studies in descriptive ethics designed to discover how men actually do think about the use of violence in various contexts. The literature of the early church has been combed by scholars such as Adolf Harnack, who wrote *Militia Christi: Die christliche Religion und der Soldatenstand in den ersten drei Jahrhunderten* (Tübingen: Mohr, 1905); C. J. Cadoux, the author of *The Early Christian Attitude to War: A Contribution to the History of Christian Ethics* (London: Headley Bros., Ltd., 1919) now out of print; and Roland Bainton, who contributed an article on "The Early Church and War" to the *Harvard Theological Review*, Vol. 39, No. 3 (July, 1946), pp. 189-212. There have been periods when the dilemmas of the use of force have been more salient for Christians. The responses given by believers occupying various social roles in different epochs should be examined carefully to help us better understand the interrelationships among doctrinal and ethical heritage, ecclesiastical organization, social locus, and the socio-political situation in determining Christian attitudes toward war and peace. Detailed studies of the reasoning and response of diverse Christian groups caught within particular historical crises would be highly profitable in helping us perceive the factors disposing people to acknowledge and observe moral restraints upon their conduct in war.

Two helpful background materials for such an enterprise would be Ernst Troeltsch's typology of religious associations set forth in his two-volume study, *The Social Teaching of the Christian Churches,* translated by Olive Wyon (New York: The Macmillan Company, 1931) and the essay by Max Weber, "Religious Rejections of the World and Their Directions," in *From Max Weber: Essays in Sociology,* translated, edited, and with an introduction by H. H. Gerth and C. Wright Mills (London: Kegan Paul, Trench, Trubner & Co., Ltd., 1947), pp. 323-59. The analytical schemes developed in these works are applied to the illumination of historical case histories in the work of David A. Martin, *Pacifism: An Historical and Sociological Study* (London: Routledge and Kegan Paul, 1965). Using the period of the English civil war of the seventeenth century as "a pilot study," Martin tests his "basic thesis: an ambivalence between the rejection of power and the acceptance of revolutionary violence" (p. x) through an examination of pacifist groups in more recent British history. In Martin's study, sociological theory is brought to bear upon historical materials in order to better understand modes of reasoning concerning the use of violence.

The British historian Maurice H. Keen focuses upon legal practice rather than ethical theory in his book *The Laws of War in the Late Middle Ages* (Toronto: University of Toronto Press, 1965). Knowledge of actual practice is very helpful in understanding the significance attached to certain criteria of the just war. For instance, pecuniary interests were at stake in determining the justice of a cause and the power of a prince to authorize a public war. "In a war fought under the avowal of a sovereign prince, the soldier could fight, and had a legal title to his gains of war" (p. 85). ". . . the first principle of the legists was that only a just war could have legal consequences . . . The justice of a war could not only render acts, which would otherwise be crimes, legitimate, it could also endow them with legal consequences . . . A war which was unjust had no standing in law, and those who took part in it had none either: 'Knights who take part in a war without just cause,' wrote Nicholas of Tudeschi, 'should rather be called robbers than knights

. . .' The legality of actions was to be judged in accordance with the justice of the cause in which they were done . . ." (p. 64 f.). If a war in which a knight participated were declared to be a legally unjust war, he not only became guilty of lese majesty, but "he could no longer pursue any claims to unpaid ransoms, *appatis*, and so on, because his actions were admitted to be outside the law, and no legal claim could arise out of an originally illegal act. This was in fact one of the regular defenses against a claim to ransom money," which was the major source of the income of medieval knights (pp. 92 f.).

The labor of historians facilitates appreciation of the thought of the major individual thinkers who have addressed themselves to the moral problem of war throughout history. The most formative influence upon Christian thought has been Saint Augustine (d. 430). *The Political and Social Ideas of St. Augustine*, a comprehensive, carefully documented study by Herbert A. Deane, available in paperback (New York: Columbia University Press, 1963), contains a chapter dealing specifically with "War and Relations Among States." Deane is properly critical of the earlier standard work, *La doctrine politique de saint Augustine*, by Gustave Combès (Paris: Librairie Plon, 1927). Although relevant passages are scattered throughout the Augustinian writings, the focal point for discussion of Augustine's understanding of the justifiable use of force is Book 19 of *The City of God*. A work that deserves mention even though it will not soon appear on local library bookshelves is the 258-page monograph by Harald Fuchs on "Augustin und der Antike Friedensgedanke," which appeared as the third number of *Neue Philologische Untersuchungen*, edited by Werner Jaeger (Berlin: Weidmannsche Buchhandlung, 1926). Part One of the work, to which my reading has been confined, is an *explication du texte* of Book 19 of *The City of God*.

Many works devoted to the thought of individual thinkers contain valuable exposition of their views upon the morality of war. Aquinas has received much attention, although his writings on war are neither extensive nor original. Joan D. Tooke is the author of *The Just War in Aquinas and Grotius* as seen through the eyes of a modern Christian pacifist (London: S.P.C.K., 1965). A very brief summary of the late scholastic thought in which the just war doctrine attained its most thorough elaboration is offered in a chapter on "War and the Law of War" in *Political Thought in Sixteenth-Century Spain: A Study of the Political Ideas of Vitoria, DeSoto, Suárez, and Molina,* by Bernice Hamilton (New York: Oxford University Press, 1963).

The Protestant Reformers could not avoid grappling with the problem of war. Luther's essays on the subject, including "Secular Authority: To What Extent It Should Be Obeyed" (1523), "Admonition to Peace" (1525), "Against the Robbing and Murdering Bands of Peasants" (1525), "Whether Soldiers, Too, Can Be Saved" (1526), and "On War Against the Turk" (1529), can be found in *Luther's Works, American Edition,* Vol. 44 (Philadelphia: Fortress Press, 1966), Vol. 45 (Philadelphia: Muhlenberg Press, 1962), Vol. 46 (Philadelphia: Fortress Press, 1967). Calvin, in a succinct section of the *Institutes of the Christian Religion,* Vol. 2: IV, 22, 11-12, edited by John T. McNeill, translated by Ford Lewis Battles (Philadelphia: The Westminster Press, 1960), pp. 1499-1501, asserts that "both natural equity and the nature of the office dictate that princes must be armed not only to restrain the misdeeds of private individuals by judicial punishment, but also to defend by war the dominions entrusted to their safekeeping, if at any time they are under enemy attack." Against the objection "that in the New Testament there exists no testimony or example which teaches that war is a thing lawful for Christians," Calvin responds that "there is no reason that bars magistrates

from defending their subjects" and that "an express declaration of this matter is not to be sought in the writings of the
apostles; for their purpose is not to fashion a civil government, but to establish the spiritual Kingdom of Christ." Calvin reiterates the restraining criteria of a just war transmitted
through the tradition (compare Thomas Aquinas, *Summa
Theologica*, II, II, Q. 40). Princes must act for a just cause:
". . . to preserve the tranquility of their dominion, to restrain
the seditious stirrings of restless men, to help those forcibly
oppressed, to punish evil deeds . . ." War must be a last
resort: ". . . surely everything else ought to be tried before
recourse is had to arms." War must be waged under public
authority and with a right intention: "But it is the duty of all
magistrates here to guard particularly against giving vent to
their passions even in the slightest degree . . . let them not
allow themselves to be swayed by any private affection, but
be led by concern for the people alone. Otherwise, they very
wickedly abuse their power, which has been given them not
for their own advantage, but for the benefit and service of
others."

The development of attitudes towards war and revolution within the Reformed Churches on the continent and
the Puritan bodies of England has been a topic of sharp
dispute. Michael Walzer, in a chapter on "Politics and War"
in *The Revolution of the Saints: A Study in the Origins of
Radical Politics* (London: Weidenfeld & Nicolson, 1966),
extends Roland Bainton's argument that later Calvinists reverted in practice to the conception of the crusade. The
military style of the crusader, typified by Saint Barnard, was
"recapitulated in the hundred years of Protestant militancy
that stretched roughly from the 1550's to the 1650's. The cul-
minating point was reached in Cromwell's England. For if
the political analogue of the just war was the limited act of
legal resistance, then the analogue of the crusade—once the

nation had replaced the world of Christendom—was revolution. Behind both crusade and revolution lay the idea of
contention for a cause. It was at revolution that Calvinist
thinkers finally arrived, by imposing their conscientious purposes upon the medieval notions of warfare" (p. 270). According to Walzer, "Puritans never adopted the Catholic insistence that war was essentially a secular affair, a matter of
fallen nature, a limited, short-term response to a specific
violation of peace and order" (p. 282). ". . . permanent
warfare was the central myth of Puritan radicalism" (p. 290).
Puritan preachers brought about "the erosion of traditional
notions about the just (limited) war" (p. 290). Their crusading, revolutionary zeal was fed by "an increasingly secure
feeling that the saints did know the purposes of God, a more
open and direct reinforcement of their pride and conten-
tiousness" (p. 291). It would be helpful to compare Puritan
practice with a larger portion of "the Catholic tradition"
than is represented by a passage Walzer quotes from Suárez:
"War is permissible only that a state may guard itself from
molestation" (p. 269). What were Catholics doing while
Puritans, in their pride and self-certainty, were subverting
moral restraints upon the use of force? By Walzer's account,
"Catholic priests and laymen, engaged in political activity,
tended in their tactics toward assassination plots and old-
fashioned conspiracies revolving around great noblemen"
(p. 131). Walzer notes that assassination was a form of
political use of violence that was "specifically ruled out by
most Calvinist writers" (p. 239). Why? Why were the new
Puritan crusaders squeamish on this point when the presumed upholders of the uncorrupted just war reasoning were
less so? Whatever the status of the *jus ad bellum* in the
respective camps may have been, it would be helpful to have
detailed studies of the assessments made of particular types
of acts that would fall under the *jus in bello*. Both categories

form part of the traditional just war doctrine. To what extent
are they separable in thought and practice? Hugo Grotius
was, according to Pompe, "the last great exponent of the
Christian doctrine of war." "After Grotius the doctrine of
natural law and just war gradually fell into decay." There
followed a prolonged "period of indifference" (*Aggressive
War*, p. 141). It was not until the end of the nineteenth
century, and especially with the outburst of massive warfare in the twentieth century, that a new "period of discrimination" appeared in which scholars sought to recover
the fundamental ideas of the just war doctrine and overcome
its practical deficiency by inventing new institutional forms
useful in the prevention, melioration, and punishment of
war.

It is not easy to find adequate surveys of the history of
pacifist thought. In his small volume, *Christian Pacifism in
History* (Oxford: Basil Blackwell, 1958), Geoffrey F. Nuttall
observes that "to offer a straight narrative history of Christian
Pacifism would hardly be possible. The story is too discon-
tinuous, the existence, or at least the appearance, of pacifists
and pacifist witness within the Church is too occasional
and sporadic" (p. 1). There are, of course, histories of individual pacifist leaders and their movements from New Testament times, through medieval sects, to the post-Reforma-
tion emergence of the historic peace churches—Mennonites,
Quakers, and the Church of the Brethren—and on to contemporary, secular variations of pacifist belief. Three recently
published anthologies include writings of an assembly of
Christian and non-Christian pacifists of diverse backgrounds
and modes of thinking. Although they pursue different logics,
they are placed in the elastic category of pacifist and appear
side by side in *The Pacifist Conscience*, edited by Peter
Mayer (New York: Holt, Rinehart and Winston, 1966); *In-
stead of Violence: Writings by the Great Advocates of Peace*

and Nonviolence Throughout History, edited by Arthur and Lila Weinberg (New York: Grossman Publishers, Inc., 1963); and *The Quiet Battle,* edited by Mulford Q. Sibley (Garden City, N. Y.: Doubleday & Company, Inc., 1963).

In *Christian Pacifism in History* Nuttall contributes to an appreciation of the variety of beliefs held by pacifists by leading readers along "the various avenues they have traversed to reach their pacifist convictions." He seeks the "inner principle" of five different types of Christian pacifism in chapters entitled "The Fear of Idolatry," "The Law of Christ," "The Ministry of Suffering," "The Dignity of Man," and "The Means of Redemption." Nuttall notes that the "five titles are thus meant to indicate some of these avenues: the approaches which were made use of by the early Christians in the first three centuries; by a variety of sects in the Middle Ages; by the Swiss Anabaptists and Dutch Mennonites in the sixteenth century; by the English Quakers in the seventeenth century; and lastly by our own approach in the twentieth" (p. 3).

The title of a chapter in *War, Peace, and Nonresistance* by the Mennonite scholar, Guy Franklin Hershberger (Scottdale, Pa.: The Herald Press, 1944), significantly draws the line between "Biblical Nonresistance and Modern Pacifism." "Nonresistance and pacifism are both Scriptural terms, taken from the Sermon on the Mount. The former is taken from the words of Jesus, 'Resist not him that is evil.' The latter comes from the words, 'Blessed are the peacemakers.' In the Latin Bible the word for peacemakers is *pacifici,* the direct English form of which is *pacifists* . . . The term nonresistance as commonly used today describes the faith and life of those who accept the Scriptures as the revealed will of God, and who cannot have any part in warfare because they believe the Bible forbids it, and who renounce all coercion, even nonviolent coercion. Pacifism, on the other hand, is a term which covers many types of opposition to war. Some modern pacifists are opposed to all wars, and some are not. Some who oppose all wars find their authority in the will of God, while others find it largely in human reason. There are many other differences among them. It is therefore important to attempt a classification of modern pacifists, and to compare and evaluate their philosophies" (p. 203). Hershberger concludes the chapter, in which he treats international peace plans, Quaker pacifism, liberal Protestant pacifism, pacifism and the social gospel, twentieth-century pacifism, nonviolent resistance, Tolstoy, Gandhi, and the political objector to war, with a section "Difficulties of Classification." He notes that "the types here outlined overlap to some extent . . . The Biblical nonresistant is the easiest to identify and classify. He renounces war because it is contrary to the teachings of the Scriptures, and he holds aloof from such activities of the state as are associated with methods of compulsion . . . Among other pacifists, classification is more difficult" (pp. 230 f.).

In focusing upon the sixteenth-century history of the left wing of the Protestant Reformation, George Hunston Williams, in his volume *The Radical Reformation* (Philadelphia: The Westminster Press, 1962), is able to distinguish "at least four kinds of opposition to warfare in the Radical Reformation as a whole. There was the Erasmian prudential pacifism, which saw war as wanton and futile, with a truly just war as very rare and even then usually avoidable . . . There was, secondly, the evangelical pacifism of conventicular separatism (Grebel) based upon Dominical counsels in the Gospel. Thirdly, there was the suffering pacifism which sought out in persecution and martyrdom from 'worldly Christians' a confirmation of their elect faith. And, finally, there was the closely related provisional and suffering pacifism which, while accepting the daily cross including even death, stressed the eventual compensation or vindication in the quite bloodly eschatological warfare of the saints as fore- seen by the seer of The Revelation and other apocalyptists ancient and medieval" (p. 226). Williams' volume contains fascinating examples of pacifist casuistry. For example, the eighth resolution passed by a synod convened by Menno Simons at Wismar in November, 1554, "permitted Anabap- tists on a journey to carry a saber or sword as a matter of elementary precaution against robbers, but only as camou- flage, for it was not to be employed" (p. 488). Both the problem and the solution are familiar to latter day advocates of nuclear deterrence. Williams observes that the "same ar- ticle permitted Anabaptists who were called up for watch and ward and other duties to present arms at the regular inspections, but, again, they were not to use them" (pp. 488 f.).

Pacifist history, thought, and action do not stand in the same relationship to the major academic disciplines as does the just war tradition. One does not encounter frequent allusions to pacifist sources in works in international law, political philosophy, arms strategy, or even in academic ethics outside of certain seminaries. Pacifists have created their own network for communication, cooperation, and the dis- tribution of literature. Special bibliographies have been pre- pared, such as the *Bibliography of Books on War, Pacifism, Nonviolence and Related Studies,* revised edition, compiled and edited by William Robert Miller, (Nyack, N.Y.: Fel- lowship of Reconciliation, 1961) along with innumerable more ephemeral booklists and catalogues of literature avail- able by mail from groups such as the Fellowship of Recon- ciliation, and the American Friends Service Committee and many denominational agencies. *The International Peace/ Disarmament Directory,* third edition, edited by Lloyd Wil- kie and Laird M. Wilcox (York, Pa.: Lloyd Wilkie, 1963) lists a multitude of groups which form part of the "peace movement."

The Fellowship of Reconciliation, the American Friends Service Committee, the Mennonite Central Committee, and, until it became defunct in 1966, the Church Peace Mission, have been among the most active producers and distributors of such literature. Among the more significant items issued by these groups are *Foreign Policy and Christian Conscience*, by George F. Kennan, with comments by Georgia Harkness, John Courtney Murray, Eugene Carson Blake, Ernest Lefever, and Stewart Meacham (Philadelphia: Peace Education Program, American Friends Service Committee, 1959) and *Therefore Choose Life: Essays on the Nuclear Crisis* (London: International Fellowship of Reconciliation, 1961) which contains contributions by Roland Bainton, Howard Schomer, John Nevin Sayre, Helmut Gollwitzer, Charles Raven, J. de Graaf, and William Robert Miller.

The Church Peace Mission, an alliance of the Historic Peace Churches and the peace fellowships of several major denominations, first published in 1953 *The Christian Conscience and War*. It sought to provide a contemporary "statement of Christian pacifism—the so-called Third Position of Amsterdam—which would try to take account of recent theological thinking as well as of the problems arising from the challenge of communism and the threat of modern total war" (p. 4). *The Word of God in the Nuclear Age: Study Papers on the Relation of the Christian Gospel to the Crisis of Nuclear Power* was published in pamphlet form and served as a preliminary study material for a Church Peace Mission Conference in Evanston in April, 1959. The Church Mission also distributed a statement entitled *A Christian Approach to Nuclear War*, drafted by members of theological faculties in the Boston area in 1959 and intended to convey proposed revisions of the "Provisional Study Document of the

World Council of Churches," *Christians & the Prevention of War in an Atomic Age* (London: SCM Press Ltd., 1961). *Fellowship,* a publication of the Fellowship of Reconciliation, is among the oldest and largest of pacifist journals. The American Pax Association, "an association of Catholics and others who seek to promote peace and to encourage the practical application of Christian principles to the question of war," began to publish a journal, *Peace,* in 1963. These and other pacifist journals provide news notes, articles, and reviews of books and pamphlets of interest to pacifists.

The most frequently cited titles include *The New Testament Basis of Pacifism,* by G.H.C. MacGregor, first published in 1936, available in paperback (New York: Fellowship of Reconciliation, 1954); *The Theological Basis of Christian Pacifism,* by Charles E. Raven (New York: Fellowship Publications, 1951); *The Dagger and the Cross: An Examination of Christian Pacifism,* by Culbert G. Rutenber (New York: Fellowship Publications, 1950), also in paperback; *The Power of Nonviolence,* second revised edition, by Richard B. Gregg (Schocken Books, 1966), first published in 1934, revised in 1959, and available in paperback; *The Enthronement of Love: Christ the Peacemaker,* by John Ferguson (London: Fellowship of Reconciliation, 1958), first published in 1950, paperback. William Robert Miller has added a volume, *Nonviolence: A Christian Interpretation* (New York: Association Press, 1964), which, in its 380 pages, gives evidence of attention to nonpacifist sources and contains an annotated bibliography.

The works just cited are popular volumes. Pacifists have also contributed significant scholarly labors. A generation of Mennonite historians have had a profound impact upon the historiography of the Reformation period, making it impossible for responsible historians to ignore the impact of the groups that constituted the "left-wing" or "radical reformation." John Howard Yoder is a Mennonite theologian, grounded in the fellowship and life of his own community of faith, who has entered into persistent conversation with Christians holding divergent attitudes toward the morality of war. Yoder's essay "Reinhold Niebuhr and Christian Pacifism" was first published as *Heerewegen Pamphlet Number One* in 1954, and appeared in *The Mennonite Quarterly Review*, Vol. 29, No. 2 (April, 1955), pages 101-117. Along with a later essay, "Peace Without Eschatology," it has been reprinted separately as "A Concern Reprint" (Scottdale, Pa.: Concern, 1961). *The Pacifism of Karl Barth* was published as a Church Peace Mission pamphlet in 1964. A lengthier treatise on *The Christian Witness to the State*, Institute of Mennonite Studies Series No. 3 (Newton, Kans.: Faith and Life Press, 1964), establishes the theological foundations upon which judgments concerning war and other matters of public policy may be grounded by modern inheritors of the Anabaptist heritage. Yoder argues that "certain concepts, such as that of the lesser evil, while illegitimate for guiding Christian discipleship, are still relevant in the elaboration of an ethic for the state. The same can be said for the traditional Catholic doctrine of the just war." After reviewing the traditional criteria of justifiable war, Yoder observes that "all such criteria are useful attempts to delimit, in terms of the function of the state, the cases in which the use of violence is the least illegitimate. That there can be a just war in the Christian sense of the word *just* or *righteous* is, of course, excluded by definition; we can make the point only negatively. When the conditions traditionally posed for a just war are *not* fulfilled, then a war is unjust to the point that even a state, resolved to use violence, is out of order in its prosecution. That is the basis of our condemnation of the atomic bomb *even for the warring state*" (p. 49).

In *The Christian Witness to the State*, Yoder refers to
the volume, *War and the Gospel* by Jean Lasserre, translated by Oliver Coburn (Scottdale, Pa.: Herald Press, 1962),
as "the most adequate theological presentation of Christian
pacifism" (p. 49). Lasserre is a pastor of the Reformed
Church of France who defends his pacifist convictions, as
Yoder noted in his Preface to the volume, "without sub-
stantial borrowing from Anglo-Saxon thought." His work is
welcomed for its possible utility in breaking up the align-
ments which hardened between pacifist and nonpacifist
Christians in the sharp debates of the 1930's and early 1940's
concerning the propriety of Christian participation in a war
to thwart the ambitions and barbarities of Adolf Hitler's
Nazi Germany.

The advent of the nuclear age, the dominance of the
issue of Vietnam, and the passage of time have brought
about a gradual shifting of the battle lines established in
the era of World War II. But the debates were so sharp and
the leading protagonists so formidable that even now some
pacifists are inclined to respond to criticism with the rebuke
that the caviling of their opponents simply echoes "the same
old Niebuhrian questions." "The same old Niebuhrian questions" are, to a great extent, "the same old Augustinian questions." They are likely to persist. Reinhold Niebuhr gave
them forceful utterance for his time in the much republished
essay, "Why the Christian Church Is Not Pacifist," which
appears as Chapter I in *Christianity and Power Politics*
(New York: Charles Scribner's Sons, 1940). Niebuhr was
most prominent among the founders of *Christianity and
Crisis*, which, on the eve of World War II, provided a counterweight in a religious journalism to the more pacifistic, non-
interventionist inclinations of *The Christian Century*. Earlier
in his career Niebuhr had identified himself with pacifist
causes and organizations. He announced his departure in

the article, "Why I Leave the F.O.R.," *The Christian Century*, Vol. 51 (January 3, 1934), pp. 17-19.

An acute summary of the liberal type of pacifist view Niebuhr thereafter attacked is given by Cecil John Cadoux in *Christian Pacifism Re-examined* (Oxford: Basil Blackwell, 1940). Cadoux gives weight to nonpacifist arguments, but concludes that "whenever I feel disposed to agree to them, and to draw the conclusion to which they point, I am held up by two stark facts which no non-pacifist argument I have ever seen helps me to surmount. One is the diabolical savagery of the acts of fighting, a savagery which makes any plea for their compatibility with Christian love an ethical farce. The other (reflected all too unmistakably in the ever-advancing size of the world's armaments) is the chronic tendency of war to beget more war" (p. 227).

Niebuhr contended also against the pacifism of the traditional peace churches. His debate with them is most memorably recorded in *The Christian and War: A Theological Discussion of Justice, Peace, and Love,* published in October, 1958, by the Historic Peace Churches and the Fellowship of Reconciliation. The pamphlet contains a statement entitled "Peace Is the Will of God," presented to the World Council of Churches in 1953 by the Historic Peace Churches and the International Fellowship of Reconciliation; a reply, "God Wills Both Justice and Peace," written by Niebuhr and Angus Dun, first published in *Christianity and Crisis,* Vol. 15, No. 10 (June 13, 1955); and a rejoinder by the European Continuation Committee of the Historic Peace Churches.

The polarization of opinion in the churches prior to and during World War II did not prevent pacifists and nonpacifists from sharing in the formulation of the "Calhoun Report," a study popularly referred to by the name of the chairman of the commission, but formally known as *The Relation of the Church to the War in the Light of the Christian Faith: Report of A Commission of Christian Scholars Appointed by the Federal Council of the Churches of Christ in America* (New York: The Federal Council of Churches, 1944). The distinguished panel of theologians concluded that "the war is an event in the providential reign of God whom we know best through Christ crucified and triumphant. For Christian faith the whole cataclysm . . . is a tragic moment in God's work of creating and redeeming man, and in man's long struggle with himself and his Creator" (p. 12).

After atomic bombs burst upon Hiroshima and Nagasaki, the Calhoun Commission was reconvened and, in March, 1946, issued *Atomic Warfare and the Christian Faith: Report of the Commission on the Relation of the Church to the War in the Light of the Christian Faith Appointed by the Federal Council of the Churches of Christ in America* (New York: Federal Council of Churches, 1946). The Commission conceded that "we have had to recognize important new light on man's part in history." It is possible "that by misdirection of atomic energy, man can bring earthly history to a premature close. His freedom, then, is more decisive and dangerous than we had suspected" (p. 20). ". . . If a premature end of history should come . . . the problem then is whether beyond the end of history God's justice and mercy are still a ground for hope, or whether the stultification of human life by a premature end is to be feared" (p. 23). Members of the Commission included Robert Calhoun, chairman, John C. Bennett, secretary, Edwin Aubrey, Roland Bainton, Conrad Bergendorff, Harvie Branscomb, Frank Caldwell, Angus Dun, Nels Ferre, Theodore Greene, Georgia Harkness, Walter Horton, John Knox, Benjamin Mays, John T. McNeill, Reinhold Niebuhr, H. Richard Niebuhr, Wilhelm Pauck, Douglas Steere, Ernest Fremont Tittle, Henry P. Van Dusen, and Theodore Wedel.

Just before the Korean War, ten members of the Calhoun Commission were joined by Paul Tillich, Arthur H. Compton, Chester Barnard, and others, to constitute a new commission, chaired by Bishop Angus Dun. They prepared *The Christian Conscience and Weapons of Mass Destruction: Report of a Special Commission Appointed by the Federal Council of the Churches of Christ in America* (New York: Department of International Justice and Goodwill, Federal Council of Churches, December, 1950).

The British Council of Churches also convened a commission which delivered its report under the title *The Era of Atomic Power: Report of A Commission Appointed by the British Council of Churches* (London: SCM Press, 1946). It was followed more than a decade later by another document, *Christians and Atomic War: A Discussion of the Moral Aspects of Defense and Disarmament in the Nuclear Age* (London: The British Council of Churches, 1959), and, in 1961, by *The Valley of Decision: The Christian Dilemma in the Nuclear Age* by T. R. Milford (London: British Council of Churches, 1961). In the meantime, the Church of England, appointed a commission to examine the first Council of Churches document and issue a report on a report. It appeared as *The Church and the Atom: A Study of the Moral and Theological Aspects of Peace and War* (London: The Press and Publications Board of the Church Assembly, 1948). The Board for Social Responsibility of the Church Assembly, in March, 1962, issued the booklet, *Modern War, What Can Christians Do Together?* Brief comments upon these and other documents emanating from the discussion in Great Britain are offered by John J. Vincent in his small paperback book, *Christ in a Nuclear World* (Manchester: Crux Press, 1962), which is useful mainly as a guide to other literature.

In every European nation churchmen have debated the morality of nuclear armaments. In Germany, a very extensive discussion centered in the 1950's upon the questions of German rearmament and the stationing of nuclear weapons upon German soil. Few American scholars or churchmen have availed themselves of the insights conveyed in the massive literature produced by continental churchmen. The continuing series of Christian Peace Conferences in Prague has provided a forum for exchange among churchmen from Eastern and Western Europe and the United States. *The Only Future* contains, as the subtitle indicates, "Documents of the Third Session of the Christian Peace Conference" (Prague: The Christian Peace Conference, 1960).

Throughout the nuclear era, virtually every major American denomination has issued statements or pronouncements pertaining to the use of armed violence in specific instances or to more general questions of the role of force in international relations. A twelve-member study commission appointed by the Methodist Church produced an extensive report entitled *The Christian Faith and War in the Nuclear Age* (New York: Abingdon Press, 1963). The National Council of the Churches of Christ has given forth pronouncements on topics such as "International Regulation and Reduction of Armaments" (1951), "The Churches' Concern in Policies Related to the Control of Armaments and of the Use of Space" (1958), and "Christian Responsibility for World Community" (1960). The National Council of Churches sponsored a "Nationwide Program of Education and Action for Peace" in 1959-60 and again in 1964-65, which coupled with a series of World Order Study Conferences, brought an outpouring of pamphlets and booklets designed to educate both laymen and clergy upon the responsibilities of the Christian with regard to international relations and the prospect of war. It cannot be said that any of these materials made a fresh contribution to ethical reflection upon the dilemmas surrounding the use of violence. They seldom exhibit a profound appreciation or even awareness of the ethical tradition of the Christian churches. The difficulties churchmen encounter in formulating pronouncements upon specific issues are analyzed in "Silence of Babel: The Churches and Peace," by Ralph B. Potter, *Social Action,* Vol. 32, Nos. 5-6 (January-February, 1966) and *Social Progress,* Vol. 56, No. 3 (January-February, 1966), pp. 34-45. The entire enterprise is subjected to sharp criticism in Paul Ramsey's book, *Who Speaks for the Church? A Critique of the 1966 Geneva Conference on Church and Society* (Nashville: Abingdon Press, 1967).

Churchmen from many nations addressed themselves to the task of defining the morality of war in the nuclear age under the auspices of the World Council of Churches. In the report of the First Assembly of the World Council at Amsterdam in 1948, a deadlock was acknowledged among those giving three different answers to the question, "Can war now be an act of justice?" It was conceded that "the churches must continue to hold within their full fellowship" not only pacifists and nonpacifists of a traditional kind but also "those who hold that, even though entering a war may be a Christian's duty in particular circumstances, modern warfare, with its mass destruction, can never be an act of justice." *Findings and Decisions: First Assembly of the World Council of Churches: Amsterdam, Holland, August 22-September 4, 1948* (New York: World Council of Churches, n.d.), pp. 54 f. This view came increasingly to be known as "nuclear pacifism." It was strongly represented within the commission which prepared the "Provisional Study Document" on *Christians and the Prevention of War in an Atomic Age— A Theological Discussion* (Geneva: Division of Studies, World Council of Churches, 1958). In discussing the question of nuclear armament, the authors, drawn from several nations and disciplines, announced, "We are agreed on one point, this is that Christians should openly declare that the all-out use of these weapons should never be resorted to. Moreover, that Christians must oppose all policies which give evidence of leading to all-out war. Finally, if all-out war should occur, Christians should urge a cease fire, if necessary, on the enemy's terms, and resort to non-violent resistance. We purposefully refrain from defining the stage at which all-out war may be reached" (Section 66).

Paul Ramsey aptly characterized the Provisional Study Document of the World Council of Churches: "In a curious way this document stands squarely within the tradition of just-war theory, and yet not so squarely there, because of an unsureness and ambiguity introduced throughout, I can only say, by the Calvinistic impulse to transform the world gone to seed in an inarticulate pacifism that has in mind at every point the final and complete prevention of war. It stands squarely within the modern Protestant movement to 'renounce' war altogether (whatever that may mean), yet not so squarely there because of the lingering force exerted by the rightfulness under certain circumstances of the just or limited war." Ramsey made the document the subject of a chapter in his important book, *War and the Christian Conscience: How Shall Modern War Be Conducted Justly?* (Durham, N.C.: Duke University Press, 1961), from which the above quotation is taken (p. 93). Ramsey's extensive writings on the morality of war have been gathered in *The Just War: Force and Political Responsibility* (New York: Charles Scribner's Sons, 1968).

Ramsey's earlier book serves as a convenient milestone marking the transition from discussion dominated by the figures and formulations of the 1930's and 1940's to the peak of the nuclear debate in which a new cast of characters would occupy prominent roles. John C. Bennett, who served as secretary of the Calhoun Commission and as an editor of

Christianity and Crisis, is among those who have spanned
the successive periods. Bennett remains among the most pro-
lific commentators upon military and foreign policy issues.
In addition to innumerable published articles and speeches,
he has contributed an essay to the book he edited on *Nuclear
Weapons and the Conflict of Conscience* (New York:
Charles Scribner's Sons, 1962) and included a chapter on
"The Ethics of Force in the Nuclear Age" in his more recent
volume, *Foreign Policy in Christian Perspective* (New York:
Charles Scribner's Sons, 1966).

Ramsey has helped Protestants recover an appreciation
of the just war doctrine. In so doing he has also stimulated
renewed conversation with Roman Catholics, among whom
there has been great ferment of thought on the issue of
war as on other matters pertaining to the church in the
modern world. Karl Hörmann, in *Peace and Modern War
in the Judgment of the Church,* translated by Mary Caroline
Hemesath (Westminster, Md.: Newman Press, 1966), reviews recent Roman Catholic teachings and debates, con-
centrating upon the work of Pius XII with mention of the
contribution of John XXIII and added references to the
early months of the pontificate of Paul VI. Extensive footnotes provide ample references to European sources.

The discussion with and among American Roman Catholics is not well covered in Hörmann's volume. The discussion
that took place before 1960 is summarized in the essays and
the extensive bibliography published in *Morality and Modern Warfare: The State of the Question,* edited by William
J. Nagle (Baltimore: Helicon Press, 1960). The volume contains the valuable essay by John Courtney Murray, "The-
ology and Modern War," originally prepared as an address
to the Catholic Association for International Peace, October,
1958. The volume *Christian Ethics and Nuclear Warfare,*
edited by Ulrich S. Allers and William V. O'Brien (Washing-

ton: Institute of World Polity, Georgetown University, 1963),
contains papers of uneven quality presented to the Second
Annual Conference on Christian Political and Social Thought
at Georgetown University in July, 1961.

Recent papal and conciliar pronouncements have provided foci for debate. The Encyclical Letter of John XXIII,
Pacem in Terris, made public April 11, 1963, alluded to the
problems of accidental war and nuclear testing, and ven-
tured recommendations concerning nuclear disarmament.

> Even though it is difficult to believe that anyone would dare
> bring upon himself the appalling destruction and sorrow that
> war would bring in its trail, it cannot be denied that the con-
> flagration can be set off by some unexpected and unpremedi-
> tated act. And one must bear in mind that, even though the
> monstrous power of modern weapons acts as a deterrent,
> there is nevertheless reason to fear that the mere continu-
> ance of nuclear tests, undertaken with war in mind, can
> seriously jeopardize various kinds of life. Justice, then, right
> reason and consideration for human dignity and life ur-
> gently demand that the arms race should cease; that the stock-
> piles which exist in various countries should be reduced
> equally and simultaneously by the parties concerned; that
> nuclear weapons should be banned and finally that all come
> to an agreement on a fitting program of disarmament, em-
> ploying mutual and effective controls (Paragraph 111 f).

Controversy flourished over the proper translation and the
import of the segment of paragraph 127 which, in the Latin,
read: *Quare aetate haec nostra, quae vi atomica gloriatur,
alienum est a ratione, bellum iam aptum esse ad violata
iura sarcienda.* In the version distributed by the National
Catholic Welfare Conference this passage, which some pacifists chose to read in the sense that "it is hardly possible to
imagine that in the atomic era, war could be an instrument
of justice," was rendered in its context, thusly:

126. Men are becoming more and more convinced that dis-

putes which arise between states should not be resolved by recourse to arms, but rather by negotiation.

127. We grant indeed that this conviction is chiefly based on the terrible destructive force of modern weapons and a fear of the calamities and frightful destruction which such weapons would cause. *Therefore, in an age such as ours which prides itself on its atomic energy it is contrary to reason to hold that war is now a suitable way to restore rights which have been violated.* Pacem in Terris: *Encyclical Letter of Pope John XXIII, April 11, 1963* (Washington: National Catholic Welfare Conference, 1963), p. 29 f.

The draft of Article 25, "On the Making of Lasting Peace," of Schema XIII, which was introduced near the close of the third session of the second Vatican Council in November, 1964, provided another focus for debate. It read:

Although, after all the aids of peaceful discussion have been exhausted, it may not be illicit, when one's rights have been unjustly hampered, to defend those rights against such unjust aggression by violence and force, nevertheless the use of arms, especially nuclear weapons, whose effects are greater than can be imagined and therefore cannot be reasonably regulated by men, exceeds all just proportion and therefore must be judged before God and man as most wicked.

Theodore Weber, in commenting upon this passage, inquires: "Does the schema mean to condemn all nuclear weapons as inherently disproportionate and uncontrollable, or only those that are judged to be so by contrast with more limited forms of nuclear arms?" Weber's question appears in an essay, "Questions for Vatican II," which, along with papers by Paul Ramsey, Walter Stein, Justus George Lawler, William V. O'Brien, and Bishop John J. Wright, is presented in a pamphlet entitled *Peace the Churches and the Bomb* (New York: The Council on Religion and International Affairs, 1965), p. 14. Weber discusses the relevance of the just war doctrine further in his pamphlet, *Modern War and the Pursuit of Peace* (New York: The Council on Religion and International Affairs, 1968).

When the "Pastoral Constitution on the Church in the Modern World" was finally adopted by Vatican II, December 7, 1965, it contained the concession, "As long as the danger of war remains and there is no competent and sufficiently powerful authority at the international level, governments cannot be denied the right to legitimate defense once every means of peaceful settlement has been exhausted" (Paragraph 79). The *jus ad bellum* and the *jus in bello* found expression in the following paragraph:

> But it is one thing to undertake military action for the just defense of the people, and something else again to seek the subjugation of other nations. Nor does the possession of war potential make every military or political use of it lawful. Neither does the mere fact that war has unhappily begun mean that all is fair between the warring parties (*Ibid.*).

The Council announced that it "makes its own the condemnations of total war already pronounced by recent Popes, and issues the following declaration: "Any act of war aimed indiscriminately at the destruction of entire cities or of extensive areas along with their population is a crime against God and man himself. It merits unequivocal and unhesitating condemnation" (Paragraph 80). *The Documents of Vatican II*, edited by Walter M. Abbott (New York: Association Press, 1966), pp. 293-294.

Passages such as these, along with the allocution of Pope Paul VI at the United Nations, October 4, 1965, have been the subject of a large number of discussions to be found in journals such as *Commonweal, America, The Catholic World,* and *worldview*. Robert W. Tucker, a political scientist on the faculty of Johns Hopkins University, subjected the teaching of Vatican Council II on war to sharp criticism in the pamphlet, *Just War and Vatican Council II: A Critique,* with commentary by George G. Higgins, Ralph Potter, Richard H. Cox, and Paul Ramsey (New York: The Council on Religion and International Affairs, 1966). Willaim V. O'Brien offers a brief critique of the work of Vatican Council II in his book, *Nuclear War, Deterrence and Morality* (Westminster, Md.: Newman Press, 1967).

Roman Catholic pacifists in an array of types and subtypes have emerged to greater prominence in the age of nuclear armament and the war in Vietnam. A thoroughgoing pacifism has long found expression in American Catholic circles through Dorothy Day and the Catholic Worker movement and through men such as Thomas Merton. The extensive writings of Gordon C. Zahn, a Roman Catholic professor of sociology holding pacifist convictions, have been gathered in a volume, *War, Conscience and Dissent* (New York: Hawthorn Books, Inc., 1967). Zahn rejects the notion that the criteria of the just war doctrine should be the norms for determining the moral permissibility of Christian participation in war. He not infrequently reiterates the criteria in goading those who profess them to observe them in practice. But the practical ineffectiveness of the just war criteria as restraints upon conduct has been a main theme in his writing.

More numerous are Roman Catholics who accept the traditional criteria of the just war, apply them in assessing current military policies, and conclude that a particular war, or, in some men's view, any war in the nuclear age is immoral. E. I. Watkin provides a compact version of what has frequently been called a "nuclear pacifist" argument in his essay "Unjustifiable War," in *Morals and Missiles: Catholic Essays on the Problem of War Today*, edited by Charles S. Thompson (London: James Clarke, 1959). Watkin asserts that "to argue that the traditional criteria of the just war are no longer relevant is patently false. Never before has their relevance been so clear, their application so easy" (p. 53). Nuclear war could not be fought with reasonable hope of victory; it would entail indiscriminant and therefore immoral means which would bring death to noncombatants; and the good probably to be achieved by victory would not outweigh the probable, *a fortiori* the certain, evil effects of the war. Justus George Lawler also begins his argument in his book *Nuclear War: The Ethic, The Rhetoric, The Reality: A Catholic Assessment* (Westminster, Md.: Newman Press, 1965) with "the assumption that the entire traditional doctrine of the just war is theoretically valid, and that it will remain theoretically valid for individual nation-states until that time when a world-wide effective political federation comes into being" (p. 29). The sharpest, most rigorous presentation of the nuclear pacifist position is given in the series of essays by British Roman Catholic scholars edited by Walter Stein and published in England under the title *Nuclear Weapons and Christian Conscience* (London: Merlin Press, 1961) and later in the United States as *Nuclear Weapons: A Catholic Response* (New York: Sheed and Ward, 1962). The argument is there pursued with relentlessness and integrity. ". . . nuclear war is not merely a catastrophic menace, but a *wickedness.*" The policy implications are stated baldly: ". . . (T)o will the means to peace in our situation is to be ready to bear very grave risks indeed (though we cannot, anyway, avoid very grave risks of one kind or another). In effect, we should have to be prepared for unilateral disarmament (or an equivalent unilateral risk-taking—whatever the diplomatic formalities) and so ultimately for non-violent resistance" (p. 142 f). The argument leads on beyond the political dimension: "Unconditional disarmament would be only the first step." The measures discussed "would acquire an essential added dimension by a revival of Western religious energies . . . Without this religious dimension, non-violent resistance seems doomed" (p. 151). Paul Ramsey contends with Stein in his essay "More Unsolicited Advice to Vatican Council II" in *Peace the Churches and the Bomb* and also in the pamphlet *The Limits of Nuclear War* (New York: The Council on Religion and International Affairs, 1963).

The nuclear pacifist position is strongly represented in the essays brought together in the volume, *Breakthrough to Peace: Twelve Views on the Threat of Thermonuclear Extermination,* edited by Thomas Merton (New York: New Directions Books, 1962) and also in the anthology, *God and the H-Bomb,* edited by Donald Keys (New York: Bellmeadows Press, 1961). Some authors have attempted to make their nuclear pacifist arguments yield judgments against indulgence in any form of warfare in the nuclear age. James W. Douglass, for example, in an article, "The Christian and Eschatological War," *Perspective: A Magazine Relating Religion to Our Times* Vol. 8, No. 3, (May-June, 1963), pp. 68-77, reasons that, "Because man has entered an eschatological context of his own making, he is forbidden to resort to any force which bears with it the clear danger of escalation into total nuclear war. But since in our shrinking world any war presents this danger . . . then it becomes clear that within the eschatological context all wars are forbidden" (p. 74).

In the mid-1960's Vietnam has dominated the headlines and the debates concerning the morality of war. A new generation of commentators and groups has arisen. But, in spite of the heralding of the "new politics" and the "new left," there is no sign of significant new variations of the basic attitudes toward war and peace outlined by Bainton. Various subtypes can be defined, but they can be readily identified as variants of pacifism, the just war theory, or the crusade. Familiarity with the history of Western thought concerning the justifiability of resort to force can help one foresee where certain paths of argumentation will lead. Such lore will not, however, enable one to escape the demand for decision on what one can or cannot do or allow to be done by one's nation in war. The possibility of grounding conscientious objection to a particular war upon respect of the criteria of the just war doctrine is explored in the essay "Conscientious Objection to Particular Wars," by Ralph B. Potter, in *Religion and the Public Order,* IV, edited by Donald Giannella (Ithaca, N.Y.: Cornell University Press, 1968).

In our review we have, for the most part, neglected the immense number of articles of extremely uneven quality that have appeared in periodicals. The overwhelming majority of relevant material has been published in *The Christian Century, Christianity and Crisis, Commonweal, America,* and *worldview.* The latter journal, a monthly publication of the Council on Religion and International Affairs, provides the widest forum for the discussion of matters pertaining to the morality of war and foreign policy.

Those who wish to share in the continuing discussion can locate new materials by consulting the *Social Sciences and Humanities Index,* formerly the *International Index,* edited by J. Doris Dart (New York: The H. W. Wilson Company); the *Index to Legal Periodicals,* edited by Mildred Russell (New York: The H. W. Wilson Company); *Arms Control and Disarmament: A Quarterly Bibliography with Abstracts and Annotations,* compiled by the Arms Control and Disarmament Bibliography Section, General Reference and Bibliography Division, Reference Department, Library of Congress; and *Arms Control and Disarmament: Studies in Progress or Recently Completed,* compiled for the United States Arms Control and Disarmament Agency by the External Research Staff, Bureau of Intelligence and Research, Department of State. The latter two documents are for sale by the Superintendant of Documents, United States Government Printing Office. To these bibliographical resources should be added *Peace Research Abstract Journal,* published in Clarkson, Ontario, by the Canadian Peace Research Institute. A variety of secular journals ranging from the *Bulletin of Atomic Scientists, Foreign Affairs,* and the *Journal of Conflict Resolution,* to *War/Peace Report* and *Liberation* may carry articles of interest or review works appearing elsewhere. *Intercom,* a publication issued seven times a year by the Foreign Policy Association, contains valuable listings of resources for the study of questions of defense and foreign policy. A large variety of voluntary associations, including church councils and denominations, issue publications in which relevant questions are discussed. Two works may be of help to those seeking a map or guide to the various schools of thought on the wide range of issues pertaining to arms policy. They are *The Arms Debate* by Robert A. Levine (Cambridge: Harvard University Press, 1963) and a more popular rendition of much of the material contained in Levine's volume: *The War-Peace Establishment,* by Arthur Herzog (New York: Harper & Row, Publishers, 1965).

A great deal of what is published is of very mediocre quality. Those who are deeply concerned might better use their time reading basic materials such as Bainton's volume and doing some hard thinking on their own. The perennial dilemmas surrounding the use or nonuse of force will not be made to disappear by finding one more article, by reading or even by writing bibliographical essays. In mastering the types of works reviewed here, one can only hope to come to a better understanding of the cost of each option and, perhaps, a keener sense of fellowship with all those who have borne the same risks of decision and action.